Money Management for Young Adults

From Your First Paycheck to Your First Million

Luke Villermin

D1600312

To those who *zig*
when others *zag*.

Contents

Introduction

It Starts with a Paycheck

In 1909, Grace Groner was born on a small farm in rural Lake Forest, Illinois. Orphaned at age twelve, Grace had humble beginnings and eventually went to work as a secretary at Abbott Laboratories, earning a modest salary for over four decades. After Grace passed away in 2010, at the age of one hundred, the town of Lake Forest discovered that she left $7.2 million to a foundation she had formed years before her death.

One simple action at the start of Grace's employment made all the difference in her accumulation of wealth. It was during her first year at Abbott that Grace purchased three shares of the company's stock for $60 each, a $180 total investment. She never bought another share, but simply held on to her original stock through thirteen recessions, wars, and countless economic downturns, never wavering from her investment strategy. With the help of dividend reinvestments, stock splits, and the natural appreciation of her shares, Grace's investment grew over time, eventually building her fortune.

The Lake Forest community was shocked when they learned of Grace's wealth because she never gave any impression that she was a millionaire. During the Great Depression, Grace learned to live frugally, and for the rest of her life she continued these habits. She lived in a small one-bedroom cottage, and it is even said that after her car was stolen, Grace walked everywhere instead of buying another vehicle. This lifestyle is not what comes to mind when most people picture a multimillionaire.

Grace's story is a reminder that wealth can be built through consistent, long-term investing and smart financial planning, regardless of income level. Like Grace, what you do with your first paychecks can have a profound impact on the direction of your life.

Money Management for Young Adults is dedicated to teaching you the principles that Grace lived by so you, too, can take control of your money and build a brighter financial future. What Grace chose to do with her first paychecks changed her life, and her legacy, forever.

Turning your first paychecks into over a million dollars does not require any special degree, a genius IQ, or a ton of work. What it does require is for you to educate yourself about the basics of money management and to live within your means, the first of which you will accomplish with the help of this book, and the second of which is completely up to you.

I do, however, want to be transparent—the transformation to financial abundance won't take place overnight. It takes time to grow wealth. The good news is that, as a young adult, you do have plenty of time on your side. And as you are about to learn, time will be a massive advantage on this journey.

As a young adult, how do you view money? Do you notice differences in the way you handle money in comparison to your friends? You are not alone. To many, money management seems to be a black box full of conflicting advice from parents, friends, media influencers, and coworkers.

Why does everyone have a different opinion? The answer to this question is powerfully revealed in Morgan Housel's best-selling book, *The Psychology of Money*. It is worth a read, but I'll summarize an important takeaway for you here: our money habits are passed down to us by our families, and the economic times of their past upbringings have an outsized influence on their unique perspective on money and how to handle it.

Quite obviously, two children—one born into poverty and the other raised with multigenerational wealth—will grow up with different habits of spending and saving. But even as we advance to adulthood, our views depend on personal experience. A person who came of age during the Great Depression would likely invest more cautiously than someone who entered the roaring stock market of the 1980s. So keep in mind that our own biases exist when it comes to money and work to educate yourself as much as possible—as you are doing now—to get all the facts before you make a financial decision.

What You Will Learn

Personal finance is—well—personal. It isn't the same for every person. People have different goals and values, which translate into money habits and strategies that are unique to their own situations. However, kind of like how a standard handful of doctor-recommended principles are the foundation for a healthy body (such as balanced diet, regular exercise, and adequate rest), there is also a set of widely accepted actions within the personal finance community that a young person should take to achieve a healthy bank account and, eventually, financial freedom.

In this book I have done my best to pool these steps into seven chapters. The steps, which are intended to be accomplished in sequential order, include:

- Budget, reduce expenses, and set realistic goals
- Build an emergency fund
- Max out your employer-matched savings plan
- Pay down high-interest debt
- Begin saving for retirement in an IRA
- Accelerate retirement savings and plan your financial independence
- Save for other goals and deploy advanced methods

Please note that this book is not going to teach you to get rich quickly, nor will it encourage you to seek ways to accomplish that futile effort. Sacrificing in the present will be required if you expect to have a greater standard of living later.

What about those stories you hear about friends of friends getting paid thousands of dollars by trading options contracts on triple-leveraged ETFs? It's all noise. You'll hear about their wins but never about the significant losses that go hand in hand with it. In reality, there are very few ways to get rich quickly, and those that do exist require a ton of work. You won't learn any of that here, but I bring it up so that you know to stay away from anything other than slow and steady—especially when it comes to managing your money after you've earned it.

Now, if you are reading this, chances are you have just started working your first "real" job; maybe you just graduated from high school and got kicked out of your parents' house to fend for yourself, or perhaps you are attending or recently finished college or trade school. Whatever the case, you now have skills to create a reliable source of income for the first time in your life. Congrats! And welcome to the world of adulting.

You may have never been taught how to manage money (we certainly know that most schools do not teach personal finance to the degree that would be helpful), and I'm sure you want to know how to handle all that cash now that you are finally raking it in. It is likely that you have heard talk of investing and saving for retirement but don't know where to start or how much to put aside for later in life. Also consider the dirty "D" word—*debt*. How do you handle it, and is it okay to have some? I'll cover all these topics in depth.

"So why is it so important that I start worrying about money while I'm young?" you might ask. "I FINALLY have cash coming in and I'm ready to SPEND it. I have been waiting my whole life for this."

Look, I get that you want to have fun. You worked hard to get where you are and now you want to live a little, go out, try trendy restaurants, buy a new car, and stock your wardrobe with designer logos. But there is a simple answer to why being young and making a plan for your money now will pay off in the future—the phenomenon of compounding.

The Magic of Compounding

Compounding plays an important role in how your money and wealth grows, and one of the most influential variables in this equation is the amount of *time* you allow it to grow. If you read my prequel to this book, *A Teenager's Guide to Investing in the Stock Market: Invest Hard Now | Play Hard Later,* you have already received a thorough lesson on what compounding is and why it is critical to start taking advantage of it while you are young, so enjoy this refresher.

If you are starting this book with no, or limited, background on investing and compounding, that's okay—I believe you will find it addressed adequately enough here to bring you up to speed on the basics.

Another note: the tactics specific to investing and growing your money are contained in about half of the chapters in this book, and compounding rates greatly impact long-term investing strategies and financial planning, which is why I bring up the topic in this book's introduction.

First, what is investing? Let's keep it simple. Investing is when you put your resources into something now so that you generate more of something later. For example, you can invest in studying now to get a degree later. You can also invest in going to the gym now to be in the physical shape you want later. And, of course, you can invest financially by purchasing things now that will generate much more money for you later. Now, back to compounding and why you want an investment that does just that.

Compounding occurs when an object's current growth is impacted by the sum of all its prior growth. If your money is invested, such as in the stock market, it will be subjected to compounding growth. This means that when your invested cash experiences compounding, your money makes you money, and then that extra money makes you even more money, and then that money makes money, which makes money, which makes more money, and this goes on and on and on over time—it is an exponential increase.

And interestingly, compounding shows that the amount of time that an investment is allowed to grow is often much more important than even the amount of initial money invested.

For example, the 10% annual compounded growth of an initial $1,000 investment would look like this:

Year 0 (starting amount) = $1,000
Year 1: $1,000 + ($1,000 x 10%) = $1,100
Year 2: $1,100 + ($1,100 x 10%) = $1,210
Year 3: $1,210 + ($1,210 x 10%) = $1,331
Year 4: $1,331 + ($1,331 x 10%) = $1,464
Year 5: $1,464 + ($1,464 x 10%) = $1,611

You'll notice that the account balance does not just increase by $100 (10% of the initial $1,000) each year. Instead, with compounding, the yearly 10% increase continues to lift up the prior growth as well. This phenomenon intensifies over time. While it may not appear overly impressive after only five years, here is a fast forward of this example to show future year-end balances:

Year 10: $2,594
Year 20: $6,728
Year 40: $45,259

The most noticeable growth in a set of compounding numbers is always going to be at the very end of the timeline—it's in the math. This is why you want to start compounding your money as soon as possible.

Of course, the percentage increase (aka rate) matters too. If you have a regular savings account at a bank, you are likely being paid interest every month; this money is also experiencing compounding. However, the interest rate paid by banks has generally been much less than the average 9.7% annual growth of the stock market.

Throughout this text, you'll find that 9.7% is the yearly compounding rate assumed in examples because this is widely accepted as what a stock investor could have reasonably earned over the past decades. Just note the quick disclaimer that this historical average does not necessarily guarantee what will happen in the future.

To help visualize how huge of an impact compounding could have on the amount of money your investments generate, check out Figure 1, which depicts a hypothetical investment account where the owner saves and invests one-tenth of their $50,000 salary ($5,000 per year), beginning at age twenty-five. Investments in the owner's account earn 9.7% annually. Because of compounding, the total interest earned quickly surpasses the amount of money that the investor ever even puts into the account. This is truly putting money to work.

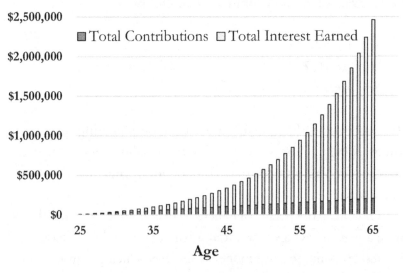

Figure 1: Compounding Investments over Time (assuming 9.7% annual return)

Other Reasons to Manage Your Money

If my spiel on compounding doesn't have you convinced on the importance of getting your money matters sorted out early, I will add in one last point—having a bunch of money when you are older isn't the only reason to get your finances in order. Also consider your mental health.

The American Psychological Association conducted a survey in 2022 that showed 72% of Americans report stressing about money at least some time each month. And according to CreditWise, finances are the leading cause of stress in Americans, occurring more often than stress about politics, work, and family.

High levels of financial stress, as with other stressors, can manifest through physical symptoms such as anxiety, compromised immune systems, headaches/migraines, high blood pressure, digestive issues, heart arrhythmia, muscle tension, depression, and a feeling of being overwhelmed.

In a similar vein, think about how money affects your personal relationships. When you are a young adult, marriage is potentially something you have entered into or are considering entering into. If so, consider this: research shows that money is the number one reason couples cite when filing for divorce in America. Think about that. Around 50% of marriages end in divorce and money is the top reason.

This stuff is important, so having a good grasp of money management can affect your relationships, happiness, and overall mental health—starting now and lasting well into your future.

The reality of not properly managing your money can manifest itself in these ways:

- **Living paycheck to paycheck:** When you don't manage your money, you might end up spending more than you earn, which can lead to a cycle of living paycheck to paycheck. This can be extremely stressful and leave you vulnerable to unexpected expenses you can't afford, such as medical bills or car repairs.
- **Debt accumulation:** Taking out loans, using credit cards, and not paying them off in full can result in a never-ending cycle of debt. This can negatively impact your credit score, making it difficult to qualify for loans or credit in the future. Additionally, the interest on these loans can accumulate, making it harder to pay off your debt in the long run.
- **Limited financial opportunities:** When you don't manage your money, you miss out on opportunities to invest in your future, such as saving for retirement or buying a house. This can limit your financial options in the future and lead to feelings of regret or missed opportunities.

To avoid ending up in these tough situations, it's important to develop a vision of consequence. This means taking a hard look at the potential repercussions of not managing your money and using that as motivation to make better financial decisions.

For example, if you don't manage your money, you might end up living a life of financial stress and struggle, which can lead to missed opportunities, such as being able to afford to travel or take time off work.

On the other hand, if you do manage your money, you can create a life of financial stability and freedom, where you have the resources to pursue your dreams and take advantage of new opportunities as they arise.

By developing a vision of consequence, you can stay motivated to make smart financial decisions, even when faced with temptation from savvy marketing or peer pressure. Ultimately, the key to managing your money is to stay focused on your goals and to make decisions that align with your vision for your future.

Now, I do want to acknowledge that for many young adults, the accumulation of money is not necessarily a primary driver in life. If you tend to agree, you likely feel more focused on defining your purpose and finding fulfillment in your work and personal life. This is fine, but it's also important to recognize that money can play a significant role in achieving these goals.

Without financial stability and security, what exactly is your plan to pursue your aspirations, unlock your full potential, and contribute everything you have to offer to society? You may still manage to accomplish goals while living paycheck to paycheck, but the odds certainly won't be in your favor.

Money can either serve as a tool to help you achieve your goals and live the life you want, or it can become a source of stress and unhappiness if you become too attached to it (either by not ever having enough, or by having an overabundance with no purpose).

Can we agree that striving toward a healthy relationship with money and getting your finances in order is a worthwhile endeavor to focus on?

Why I Wrote This Book

I wrote my first book, *A Teenager's Guide to Investing in the Stock Market* (2020), to encourage teens to start earning income and investing in what's called a Roth IRA (more on this later) as early as possible. The book received great feedback and hit the bestseller list not long after publication. However, I realize that as teenagers transition to young adulthood, they not only find themselves with more money than they've ever had, they also are surrounded by more pressure to spend that money.

In this book, I aim to lay out a practical and more holistic guide to personal finance for young people—not solely focused on investing, though that topic is certainly still heavily discussed.

What I intend is for this text to be a workable approach to managing your money as a young adult; after one bucket is filled, move your extra cash over to the next one. If you read this book cover to cover and do your best to digest it, I am certain you will walk away fully understanding the importance of saving and tracking your money. You will also have the desire to start investing your money to take advantage of compounding, ASAP.

How to Approach the Following Chapters

Your success and speed at which you accomplish this book's essential money management steps in your own life will largely boil down to two things:

1. Your income (the more money you bring in, the easier it will be to enact these steps, especially the later ones—obvious, I know);
2. Your commitment to living *below* your means.

What does it mean to live below your means? Well, living within your means implies that you are only spending money on things you can afford; basically, you aren't borrowing money to pay for what you need such as rent, food, and car insurance.

Living below your means takes it a step further—you must not buy things you want (let's say a new video game), even though you know you can afford them. This takes discipline, self-control, and good habits, but the reward is high. The more you are able to save from each paycheck, the faster you will be able to progress through the steps in this book, and the quicker you'll reach your first million dollars.

You cannot expect to make any progress on your financial situation if you do not have a handle on your spending; except for extreme situations, don't allow yourself to spend more than you make.

Living below your means is especially difficult when you are a young adult because there is no shortage of enticements for you to spend money on, coupled with the fact that your means are most likely not very high. In other words, your income is limited.

The way I recommend you approach this is to read through the book in its entirety and perform the simple exercises in each chapter. Then, leverage the road map in the back of the book to serve as your checklist for enacting these steps in the correct order.

Also, a fair warning—I've done my best to make the steps and accompanying examples in this text as relatable and easy to read as possible. However, building wealth is a slow and steady process, and excluding a handful of supernerds like myself, it is exceptionally boring to most people.

Sure, turning your extra cash into millions of dollars is exciting, but as you'll see later, it takes decades to get to that point with the average salary. That may seem too far in the future to be worth the effort, but I would argue that other than finishing this book, opening the recommended accounts and regularly funding them, and occasionally sprucing up your personal finance education knowledge, there is not much effort involved at all. Time, the collective progression of the economy, and compounding will do all the heavy lifting for you.

Buckle up and brace yourself for the most boring (but real) million dollars you've ever made. Let's dive right in.

_____

Chapter 1

Budget, Reduce Expenses, and Set Realistic Goals

What was the last thing you purchased? It may have been a good (such as a television, new mattress, or lunch), or maybe it was a service (like a plane ticket, car wash, or teeth cleaning), with payment made by one of the numerous ways to send money, such as an electronic transfer to your friend, an automatic withdrawal of your electric bill from a checking account, or a click of the Buy Now button online.

Fairly simple to recall, right? You may not remember the exact amount to the decimal point, but you likely know what you traded your money for and about how much the goods or services cost.

Now, recall what you spent money on two Saturdays ago. What was the total for the day? This might be a bit more ambitious to remember. And if I asked you to add up everything you spent last month, to the cent—*pshhh*, that's out of the question, right?

Life can be complicated, and tracking where all your money goes is sometimes tricky. However, the crucial foundation of any serious financial plan is a detailed budget that allows you to keep tabs on your money. A good budget will enable you to (1) predict how much money is coming in, (2) plan where all your money goes, and (3) check your actual performance versus the plan once time has passed.

Why Budgeting Is Critical to Success

For many people, spending money is like selecting food from a buffet. Eggrolls, fried chicken, crispy bacon, pizza, or pasta with Alfredo sauce—whatever their heart desires. But before they know it, they've lost track of what plate they're on. Things can easily get out of control at a buffet (trust me, I'm the poster child for all-you-can-eat chaos). Eventually, though, just because you *can* go back for a seventh plate doesn't mean you *should.*

Your budget should serve to keep your life in order, prevent overeating (spending), and maintain progress toward achieving your goals. When you have a budget that clearly tracks money in and money out, you are no longer flying blind, and you have the information to evaluate where you can cut spending and can form a baseline for setting realistic goals.

But alas, despite the importance of setting financial goals (as I will cover shortly), even the success of the best goal-setter will be subject to the thoroughness of their budget and rhythm of their money management habits. This is because budgeting is a system. If you want to build your wealth based on mathematics and ingenuity, rather than luck, then you must develop good budgeting skills and processes. And they must be refined.

You do not rise to the level of your goals.
You fall to the level of your systems.

—James Clear, author of *Atomic Habits*

As *Atomic Habits* author James Clear profoundly puts it: "You do not rise to the level of your goals. You fall to the level of your systems." Your money goal will be your desired outcome. Your budgeting system will be the collection of daily, weekly, and monthly habits that will get you there. Let's work on building your budget and the accompanying systems for getting the most out of it.

How to Build Your Budget

A budget will, in essence, track two things: income and expenses. Income is all money coming in. Money you earn from work as a registered nurse, profits from selling handmade jewelry, and interest the bank pays you on your savings are examples of income.

Expenses include all money going out. Your rent, what you spend on a new toy for your dog, and the money you donate to charity are all expenses. Money you put into your savings and investment accounts is also considered an expense when you are making a budget, because savings are payments to someone—yourself.

When people say they have a balanced budget, it means income (minus) expenses = $0. This is the goal. If your expenses are greater than your income this month, you've blown your budget.

Here are some common budgeting categories and brief definitions to aid you in making sure you accurately capture all information when you build your budget:

Income

- Paycheck—earned from work
- Dividends—from owning stocks
- Royalties—from others using your idea or product
- Capital gains—from assets increasing in value
- Interest—from lending out money
- Rental—from renting out a property
- Profit—from buying and selling
- Residual—continuing to get paid from past work

Expenses

- Housing—mortgage/rent, parking, maintenance
- Transportation—vehicle payments, fuel, maintenance, ride-sharing, public transport
- Food—groceries, dining out
- Debt payments—student loans, credit cards
- Personal and discretionary—household items, subscriptions, grooming, travel
- Savings—emergency fund, near-term goals, retirement
- Utilities—electricity, gas, water, cellular, internet
- Clothing
- Medical—prescriptions, copays, childcare
- Giving—gifts, donations
- Taxes—property, capital gains, income

Think about these categories and how many of them will have a place in your own personal budget. Keep in mind that the lists I provide here are far from exhaustive and are meant to serve only as a framework. Budgeting categories will vary from person to person, and there are no strict rules on where everything is bucketed as long as every dollar is accounted for.

Paying Yourself First

Pay yourself first (PYF) is a great rule to live by. It means that once you earn money, the first person you should pay is yourself. Before you pay anyone else by spending money on new clothes, food, rent, or any other bills, save money by paying yourself first. This often manifests itself as a recurring transfer set up to automatically shuttle a portion of your paycheck to a stand-alone savings account the moment it hits your checking account.

PYF keeps saving a priority and ensures that you hit your goal every month. It's like doing your future self a favor. This is not easy to do, but I have no doubt you'll be excited to watch your savings grow.

The Lowdown on Debt

It's time to talk about the "D" word. You might think of *debt* as a scary term—the truth is sometimes it is and sometimes it isn't. Debt is when you receive a good or service from someone, but you don't pay them for it at that time. When you are in debt, you are referred to as a borrower. The person you owe the money to is referred to as your lender.

Think of all the wonderful things you could own if you didn't have to pay for them at the time you purchased them. Not so fast. When you are in debt, you are simply borrowing. You have to pay for it sooner or later. You owe your lender that money. And usually, you will have to pay debt back PLUS a little more than if you had just paid the entire amount up front.

One of the most commonly used types of debt is in the form of a credit card. For example, if you use a credit card to buy a $20 pizza, you are actually using the credit card company's money to buy the pizza instead of your own. But when you pay the credit card company back later, they may require you to give them some extra money, called interest. So you might end up paying more like $24 for your original $20 pizza.

In this example, interest makes you lose money. Interest can also be a good thing, of course, when you are on the other side of the equation. For example, when you are saving money with a bank, they will pay you interest because they are able to loan your money out to others.

Sometimes, it might make sense to borrow money to get some of the larger and more expensive items that you need as you go through life. Borrowing money for a specific purpose is usually referred to as a loan. Here are some types of loans:

- Mortgage—a loan used to purchase a home or land
- Auto loan—used to purchase a car or truck
- Student loan—money borrowed to pay for education, like going to college
- Personal loan—money you can borrow to use for a variety of purposes such as paying for home improvements or a wedding

If you get a bank to loan you money for any of these purposes, you are now in debt to the bank. Remember, most debt must be paid back in its full original amount plus some additional money so that your lender gets paid for the service it provided to you. However, you usually don't have to pay the debt back all at once—it is broken into smaller amounts (bills) that you pay over a longer period.

Go with the (Cash) Flow

You may sometimes hear a person talk about their cash flow. Your cash flow can be calculated by taking your income and subtracting your expenses over a set period of time. If you bring in $6,000 per month and your expenses are $5,000 per month, then for that month you are cash flow positive. If your cash flow is negative, you are likely living paycheck to paycheck, with no wiggle room in your budget.

Most people monitor their personal cash flow to make sure their expenses are going to be fully covered when their paycheck is deposited. When I am reviewing my budget, I track my cash flow for one main reason—to make sure I do not overdraft my checking account. I have elected to treat my checking account as a pseudo "flash account" where the ins and outs of my budget all come together twice a month.

One day after a paycheck is posted in my checking, my expenses kick in to gobble it up. First are my PYF accounts (for example, savings and retirement account), which I have set up to automatically pull the budgeted dollar amounts to their destinations. Then comes my housing payment (if it's the first of the month). Next, my credit card—which is set to pay the statement balance in full—automatically takes its share.

In my budget, the timing and amount of my expenses must be able to be covered by my biweekly paychecks. To handle this in practice, I have adjusted the pay date of my primary credit card so that it does not line up with the same paycheck as the one my rent payment is relying on. This balances out the timing of my expenses. If I tried to pay rent, fund my savings accounts, and pay off my entire month's worth of groceries, utilities, and gas spending via my credit card with one single after-tax paycheck, I would be cash flow negative for those two weeks.

The simple math in Table 1 is a quick way for you to figure out how to best time your expenses and balance your cash flow.

Table 1: Sample Cash Flow Optimization

	1st of month	15th of month
Cash Into Checking Account		
Paycheck (after tax witholdings, insurance premiums, 401(k) contributions, etc.)	$1,600	$1,600
Side Hustle Profit	$280	$ —
Cash Out of Checking Account		
Rent (paid direct to landlord)	$1,100	$ —
Utilities	$ —	$172
Credit Card Bill (full statement balance; includes all other budget items not listed)	$ —	$1,125
Vehicle Payment	$425	$ —
Student Loan Payment	$ —	$267
Savings Account Automatic Transfer	$50	$50
Roth IRA Automatic Transfer	$275	$ —
Cash In - Cash Out (Target = $0)	**$30**	**$(14)**

Planning what your own cash flow looks like can be as simple as mine:

- Step 1: Estimate how much cash will be hitting your account and how frequently. Often, this is your net paycheck; your gross pay is what your employer pays you *before* withholding taxes.
- Step 2: List your expenses and their due dates. For those that are flexible on timing (such as many credit cards), fit them into the period with more breathing room.
- Step 3: Tweak until you find that your income equals your expenses.

Consider leaving some buffer so that variations in either your income or your spending will not derail this process. I also keep a layer of cash in my checking account to avoid overdraft fees by cushioning against unforeseen timing issues or unexpected use of my debit card.

Methods and Processes for Tracking Money

While you can certainly try to keep your budgets written out in a notebook or on sheets of looseleaf, things might get a little cluttered after a while. Instead, consider using online budgeting software and apps such as Mint, EveryDollar, or Goodbudget. Many of these budgeting programs will allow you to link your bank accounts and credit cards to easily pull in spending data, usually as soon as you pay. If you do this, you may not need to worry about keeping your receipts anymore (unless you want to return something).

If the idea of linking your bank accounts to an app makes you uneasy, you can always build your own budget tables on a computer with Google Sheets or Microsoft Excel. You can wait until the end of the month to update your actual numbers. But there's also nothing wrong with typing in your spending each time you buy something, instead of waiting until the end of the month to adjust.

I personally enjoy using the website and app for Empower (formerly Personal Capital) to pull in my accounts and aggregate all my expenses. The software allows me to set a spending target for the month and plots my performance versus this benchmark.

If you are like me, your monthly expenses may vary from month to month. For example, you need to rent a tux for your friend's wedding next month, or you need to have all four of your car's tires changed out, or you are booking flights for spring break.

These are all sizable, one-off expenses. These will cause variations in your budget. To account for this, I like to budget my expenses based on my last six months of actual purchases, which can be easily tracked with an aggregator such as Empower. The average of these most recent six months is what I assume my expenses will be next month, and if this number is too high, I evaluate where I can cut back spending.

Ideally, your budget would enable you to make adjustments and learn from your past experiences, both successes and failures, adjust for what works, and align for next month (take a look at Figure 2). Just like how a car's driver can glance at the dashboard to monitor how many more miles' worth of gas the tank is holding and then determine to either cut the detour from their route or seek to refuel at a station, we should be able to glance at our budgets to determine if we need to start to slow down on our spending or work on earning more income.

After all, a budget is a plan. Making a plan is one thing. Sticking to it is another. It's helpful to look back at a month's budget after the month has ended. This way, you can learn what you estimated correctly, and learn what you may need to change for next month. Often, we make a best guess when we create a budget—in reality, after taxes or fees, the amount of money you ended up spending may be different from what you estimated and planned for.

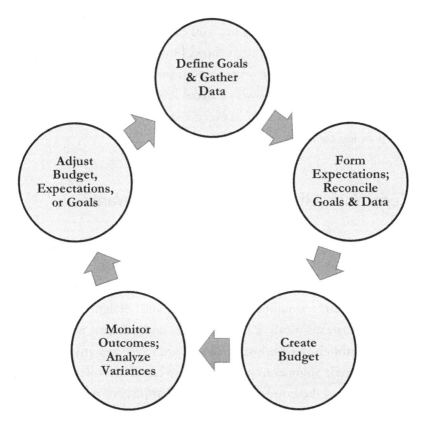

Figure 2: The Iterative Steps for Successful Budgeting

As you start earning, spending, and saving more money, you'll soon realize that these types of price variances are common in life. To keep track of all the changes, hold onto your receipts after you make a purchase (either paper printout receipts or online ones sent to your email address). This way, you can take some time each month to record your actual income and expenses. Then, when you create next month's planned budget, you can also use these new numbers.

Banks and credit unions will give you dated receipts when you deposit and withdraw money, and stores will provide a dated receipt when you buy something. When you earn money by working a job, you will receive a pay stub that shows how much you've earned and through what time period you earned it (let's say June 1 to June 15). If you get paid in cash, however, make sure to record it somewhere. You may not get a pay stub in every instance. Write cash payments down or log them on your computer.

Keep Yourself Honest—Needs vs. Wants

When you're thinking about buying something, consider this: Do you *need* it or do you *want* it? Needs are items that are required to live life—for example, food, shelter, and clothing. And I don't mean five-star restaurants, a mansion, and designer jeans. I'm talking nutritious meals, a livable house, and a decent wardrobe to get you through the workweek. Wants are really just anything that we don't need. Some examples are luxury cars, bottomless mimosas at brunch, and the hottest pair of shoes that just got released.

As you can see, needs are, well, necessities. You can't live without them, so it's unreasonable to expect someone to stop spending money on them. Wants, however, should be funded only by your leftover money—after needs are covered, and after savings are stashed away. When it comes to choosing what to do with your money, needs and savings should always be prioritized above wants. It's the best way to meet your goals in life. Remember to pay yourself first.

As a young adult, aim to only spend 80% or less of your income; what is left over after necessary expenses are paid will be put to work with the subsequent steps in this book. A commonly cited rule of thumb is to budget according to the 50-30-20 strategy, which means you allocate 50% of your paycheck toward the things you need, 30% toward the things you want, and 20% toward savings and investments.

If the analysis of your past six months of expenses reveals that you have been spending more than 80% of your income, you should make a plan to either increase your income or decrease your expenses.

Ideas for Increasing Income

To loosen some of the tightness in your budget, consider working to increase the amount of money you have coming in every month. While increasing your income will never be easy, you might surprise yourself with how creative you can be. Find something at the intersection of what you are skilled at, what people are willing to pay for, and what you are reasonably happy doing, and voilà—there's your opportunity to make some extra cash with a side hustle. Examples might be these:

- Open an online store.
- Drive for a rideshare company.
- Sell your gently used items (books, CDs, video games).

- Teach a course.
- Advertise on social media.
- Build a monetized blog.
- Rent out your property.
- Start a lawn care business.
- Provide freelance writing, photography, or design services.
- Sell baked goods.
- Become a virtual assistant.
- Become a referee or umpire at local games.
- Offer pet walking or sitting or house-sitting services.
- Volunteer for extra shifts at work.
- Ask for a raise or promotion.

Despite being at the end of the list, these last two should probably be your first approach to increasing your income since they are the lowest hanging fruit. Evaluate what can be done to squeeze more money out of your current job. If it has been a while since you received a raise or promotion, tell your manager you'd like to connect to review your compensation and go prepared with compelling bullet points that concisely list your recent accomplishments at work.

Oh, and just in case it needs saying, don't mention what your coworkers make or any personal reason for needing more money. That usually doesn't go over too well.

Ideas for Decreasing Expenses

The first step for decreasing your expenses has already been discussed ad nauseam—making a budget. Your new budget will shed light on where you have been spending too much money and will (I hope) cause your subconscious to kick in and remind you of this every time you are about to overspend.

After building a detailed budget, check if you can use some of these tactics to draw down your expenses even lower:

- Cancel subscriptions you're not using.
- Split rent with a roommate.
- Shop around for cheaper car insurance or raise the deductible.
- Cook and eat at home rather than at restaurants.
- Shop with a list to reduce impulse spending.
- Use discount codes and coupons.
- Unsubscribe from email newsletters and catalogs.
- Plan free activities.
- Reduce electricity bills by replacing incandescent lightbulbs with LED lightbulbs.
- Buy gently used clothing or shop discount stores online or in person.
- Cut back on or quit vices like smoking, drinking, and gambling.
- Use public transportation instead of driving.
- Take shorter, cooler showers.
- Carpool to work.
- Do your own nails instead of getting a salon manicure.
- Brew coffee at home.

In addition to exploring these actions, consider switching up how you actually pay for your expenses. One MIT study found that buyers paying via a credit card spend more than twice as much as cash buyers. This is because credit cards disconnect the consumption transaction, which is pleasant, from the payment transaction, which is painful. (Also, some merchants will charge you extra fees for using a credit card to pay instead of opting for cash, so be wary.)

Regarding credit cards, "When you're consuming, you're not thinking about the payments, and when you're paying, you don't know what you're paying for," said Drazen Prelec, associate professor of marketing at MIT's Sloan School of Management.

If it seems difficult to wrangle in your spending on your first few budgeting attempts, try making the switch to paying completely with cash, if you aren't already.

As mentioned earlier, there is a big psychological component to handling money, especially how we spend it. Life events and upbringing have molded us into who we are today, and it is good to be aware of your biases and tendencies.

We have learned to dance the dance we're shown, following the financial habits and beliefs of those around us. However, if we want to improve our financial situation and achieve our long-term goals, we need to start thinking differently. We need to be willing to question our beliefs about money, explore new ways of managing our finances, and take calculated risks to grow our wealth. It may be time to start dancing to a different tune.

If you love shopping and spending, you are likely to be more carefree and focused on the present. You may only see green lights when making shopping decisions and probably rarely feel any sting from making purchases. People who are frugal and strict about saving, on the other hand, often experience a lot of distress when they are considering spending—even when it comes to paying for needs. I myself fall into this category. At times, I have been so paralyzed at the thought of spending money, even when I could clearly afford it and it was classified as a need, not a want.

At the end of the day, it is important to recognize your own personality and how it impacts your spending. The goal is to stick to your budget, after all. An accurate and well-thought-out budget will give you permission to spend money on some of your wants and certainly on all of your needs. Balance your budget, and also find the balance between overspending and obsessive frugality.

Prioritize Your Expenses

Okay, so once you start outlining your income and expenses for your budget, you may come across something unsettling: your expenses are as low as they can reasonably go, and your income still does not cover them each month. If you find yourself in this situation, even for a short time, it is typically recommended to pay for your necessary expenses in this order:

1. Pay rent/mortgage (including renters' or homeowners' insurance, if required).
2. Buy food/groceries (depending on the severity of your situation and needs, you may wish to prioritize utilities before this one).
3. Pay for essential items and utilities (electricity, water, heat, toiletries, as examples).
4. Pay income-earning expenses (necessary transportation expenses, internet/phone, anything required to continue earning income).
5. Pay for healthcare (health insurance and healthcare expenses).
6. Make minimum payments on all debts and loans (student loans, credit cards, wherever you owe).

While you are doing your best to cover these bills, be vigilant in your search for ways to increase your income and decrease your expenses. It will be the only way to break out of the exhausting cycle of living paycheck to paycheck.

Set Realistic Goals

When was the last time you put your energy into reaching a goal and you met it? Think about how great it made you feel and how confident you became. As soon as we reach one goal, the next goal becomes more likely to be met as well. Success runs off momentum. Once you get the freight train rolling, not much can slow it down.

Goal-setting in your financial life is an especially important process, and, no, you don't have to wait until New Year's to do it. Many financial goals revolve around meeting a spending milestone (such as buying a new car or house) or net worth target (reaching $1 million), but can also be related to the process of growing money (let's say you take the leap into real estate investing, starting a business, or patenting a new invention).

Personal finance heavyweight Dave Ramsey offers these five steps to increasing the probability of reaching your money goals:

1. Make them specific.
2. Make them measurable.
3. Give yourself a deadline.
4. Make sure they're your own goals.
5. Write them down.

If your goals are too vague, you won't actually know how to reach them or even if you have met them. Instead of the goal, "I want to make a budget," consider, "I will make a balanced budget that forces me to pay myself first."

In a similar vein, making your goal quantifiable will certainly enable you to know once you've achieved it. Now, your budgeting goal becomes, "I want to make a balanced budget that forces me to pay myself first with 20% of my income going toward savings."

To combat the ever-present allure of procrastination, make your goals time sensitive: "I want to make a balanced budget that starts tracking my money beginning the first of next month and forces me to pay myself first with 20% of my income going toward savings."

It is also a good idea to reflect on why you want to achieve this goal. If it is because other people are doing it, reevaluate. A goal of saving to buy a BMW just because your neighbors have one may not be the best idea, especially if cars don't make the top five list of things you most appreciate in life.

And last, write down your goals. Study after study has shown that you are more likely to reach a goal if you record it with good old pen and paper and keep it where you can see it regularly. Even on a vision board. You can see a generalized view of common financial goals in Table 2 to serve as a starting place for your goal-setting process.

Along with this budgeting example, here are a few more hypothetical money goals that meet Ramsey's criteria:

- "I will max out my Roth IRA investment account by the end of this year by contributing $6,500 to it and investing it in an S&P 500 index fund to grow money tax-free for retirement."

- "I will save $10,000 each year for the next five years for the down payment on a new house by setting up an automatic transfer of $417 from each biweekly paycheck to a separate savings account."
- "I will reach financial independence by age forty by growing my passive income streams by $500/month each year, allowing me to live off $5,000/month within ten years without actively working."

Table 2: Common Financial Goals by Timeline

Timeline	Example Goals
Short term	Make a balanced budget
	Pay off credit card debt
	Start an emergency fund
Medium term	Buy a house
	Pay off vehicle
	Save for advanced degree
Long term	Achieve financial independence
	Secure retirement
	Pay for children's college

The goal of reaching financial independence by forty can certainly be considered an umbrella goal, where breaking it down further is likely helpful. This will be the case for many of your long-term financial goals. For example, your subgoal for this year may be "I will generate $500/month in passive income by the end of this year by monetizing an online cooking blog where I share my grandma's secret recipes." Thanks, Grandma!

At the end of this chapter, you will find a Financial Goals Worksheet where you can list what you are aiming to accomplish. You may already have a good idea of what you need to do to get into better financial shape and can write a few things down now, but don't forget to revisit the worksheet after finishing the book because you may have more goals to meet by then. Print out that page and tape it to your mirror, keep it on your desk, or fold it inside your wallet—as long as it's somewhere you will see it regularly. Printable worksheets are available for download on my website at **www.investnowplaylater.com/worksheets**.

In summary, creating a budget is fundamental to being on sound financial footing; before you can even begin to think about how to grow your money, you need to know where it's all going. Budgeting helps you clearly see the money you have coming in versus the money going out, and signals you whether you need to increase income, decrease expenses, or a bit of both.

Now that I have laid the foundation of money management and gotten you into a mindset of thriftiness, it's time to introduce the next step to make sure that when things go wrong in your life (and heads up, they will eventually), you won't have to derail the progress you have made toward your goals.

Key Takeaways

- Building a personal budget, along with outlining the systems you'll stick with to make the most of it, are the first and most crucial steps in managing your money once you have a steady source of income.

- After finding out where your money is going, push yourself to cut expenses deeply, especially those in the wants category, which are not necessary to survival and well-being.
- Listing your financial goals in a specific, measurable, and deadline-driven manner will increase the likelihood of your meeting them.

Take Action: Financial Goals Worksheet

Use this worksheet to identify your top financial goals. Writing down your goals will force you to clearly define them, set measurable targets, and visualize a path to success.

EXAMPLE

Goal Name: <u>Buy House</u>

Description: <u>Save enough for a 20% down payment on a house</u>

How Will I Measure Success: <u>Save $70,000</u>

Deadline: <u>10 years from today</u>

Goal Name: _____

Description: _____

How Will I Measure Success: _____

Deadline: _____

Goal Name: _____

Description: _____

How Will I Measure Success: _____

Deadline: _____

Goal Name: _____

Description: _____

How Will I Measure Success: _____

Deadline: _____

Goal Name: _____

Description: _____

How Will I Measure Success: _____

Deadline: _____

Want a free printable copy of this worksheet?
Visit investnowplaylater.com/worksheets

Chapter 2

Build an
Emergency Fund

Have you ever had a car break down on you? It happens to us all eventually, and repairs aren't cheap. The average unexpected vehicle repair will set you back about $500. Ouch!

Follow-up question: Would you be able to come up with that amount of money if this scenario were to happen to you tomorrow? If you cannot cover it with what is in your checking or savings accounts, you may be in a bind, especially if you have to put the repair bill on a credit card and cannot pay it off in full when the statement is due next month.

This hypothetical problem happens every day to many people, and, unfortunately, 56% of Americans cannot cover a $1,000 emergency expense with savings according to one Bankrate survey (Figure 3 shows this). The best way to prepare for these inevitable problems is to build an emergency fund. By thinking proactively, not reactively, you avoid getting derailed while working toward your goals.

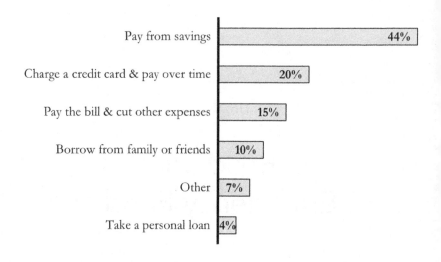

Figure 3: How Americans Would Cover an Emergency $1,000 Bill

A stash of extra money can act as a cushion to insulate you from unforeseen expenses and can keep these surprises from ruining the rest of your financial plan. That is why money management step number two, after building a budget and paying for your needs, is to put aside a small emergency fund.

How much money should this be? Many experts recommend either $1,000 or one month of expenses, whichever is greater. And once you have the money for your emergency fund, stash it away somewhere safe—safe from other people and from yourself. You don't want to spend it unless it is truly an emergency because, guess what? As soon as your emergency fund is depleted, you must work to immediately fill it back up again for the next time something inevitably rolls around.

Keep the money in a savings or checking account specifically for this purpose. If your bank is high-tech enough to enable you to divvy up your money into different buckets and label them, create one for this purpose and title it "Emergency Fund—EMERGENCY USE ONLY." The money should be easy enough to access when you finally need it, but not too easy. This is why keeping it in a separate account (or bucket within your account) is recommended.

With your budget now well on its way, calculating your one month of expenses should be a breeze. Sum up everything considered a need (such as rent, groceries, utilities, medical expenses) as well as some select discretionary items (internet, car payment, fuel, phone, subscriptions). The sum of these is called your living expenses, and if you have this amount set aside in your emergency fund, you may find yourself very thankful if you experience sudden job loss or are incapacitated and unable to work.

The goal here is to create a buffer—a shield for your bank account—to protect against sudden expenses. You don't want to have to resort to a high-interest payday loan or rack up credit card debt when you find yourself in a situation when you need to pay for something urgently. Building this emergency fund requires a specific skill—the ability to SAVE.

Getting into the Saving Mentality

Many of the people whom we consider to have an unhealthy relationship with money have something in common: they view money as having only one use—to be spent.

When you think about how the majority of people were taught money management as children, this makes sense. When you are brought up in a household and education system that does not discuss how money is obtained, you only see the other half of the equation, when it is spent. And over time, this narrow view of how money works often manifests itself in the mentality that money is limitless (except it isn't) and that money must be spent as soon as it is obtained.

This is shortsighted, however, and an unfortunate deficiency of so many people's experience in formal education. Money has another purpose—to grow, multiply, and make more of itself. This idea, the concept of leveraging the money you have now to create even more money later, is what many discussions in the rest of this book are centered around. But in order to save money into a special emergency fund, you must understand the concept of delayed gratification and be willing to deploy it in your daily life, particularly when it comes to having the strength to say no to purchases now because you know it is the right thing to do for your financial future.

If you are a person who struggles to save money, the development of your budget will likely give you the best chance at breaking free from overspending habits. But once the budget is complete, and you take it seriously, there are a few additional psychological tricks that may help you keep your emergency fund savings goal on track.

Survival of the Thriftiest

Going back to the discussion around needs and wants in chapter 1, aim to consciously ask yourself before you buy something whether you really need it to become the best version of yourself. If you don't purchase it, will it have an impact on your life five years from now? For example, if you don't buy a textbook for school and it reduces your test scores and thus your GPA, then, yes, the cost of the textbook lends itself to being a necessary expense (a need) because it could have an impact on what your life looks like in five years.

However, do you think paying for a $5 venti vanilla latte at the coffee shop will change your life for the better five years down the line? No. Especially not when you can sub out for a homemade cup of coffee for $0.25 and still get the same caffeine fix. Typically, your goals are worth more than a quick indulgence; it just boils down to where your priorities lie.

Sometimes, however, being thrifty does not mean buying cheaper. For example, if your pair of discount-brand work shoes cost $30 but you end up wearing a hole through the bottom of them every six months, you will spend $180 on shoes in the next three years, and you probably won't be too comfy either. Instead, you could maybe purchase a nice mid-tier brand for $150 and, in my experience, they'll last three years. My budget would rather choose the latter option.

Now, it is important to realize, though, that as price increases, quality often increases only to a point. Eventually, you are paying for brand status and name recognition, not quality. The average $200 leather handbag should last a good ten years with regular use and decent care. So that means a certain company's $5,000 designer handbag (you know which brand I'm talking about) should last a proportional 250 years, right?

Do your research before making a purchase, ask yourself how much use you will get out of it, and think through the purchase decision logically, not emotionally.

Betrayed by Benjamins

You may be familiar with the feeling called "buyer's remorse," which comes about when you regret making a purchase because it doesn't work or make you feel the way you expected it to. Spending money can often be an emotional experience. In fact, many emotional spending triggers commonly stem from feelings of jealousy, guilt, fear, sadness, or achievement.

When shopping, we start to tell ourselves, "If I just had this," or "If I just had that," or "I really deserve a new—," in expectation that it will make us happy. Try to recognize when this feeling is setting in so that you can avoid going down a slippery slope of overconsumption.

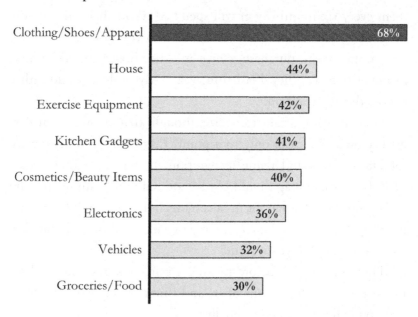

Figure 4: The Most Common Items for Buyer's Remorse; Percentage of Respondents Who Reported Regretting a Purchase in the Categories

When you are planning to make a purchase, think about why you need (or want) to buy this thing. Spending money for the wrong reason is a prescription for nausea, especially when it comes to more expensive items. For example, if you feel pressured to go out with your friends for dinner at a restaurant you know you can't afford, it might be a good idea to say no or suggest something within your budget. Why? Because, if you go through with it and wake up staring at the bill for a steak and chicken fajita plate, queso for the table, a tequila shot, and dos house margaritas, your wallet may be experiencing an even worse hangover than you are.

Many things we do in life that are bad for us feel good in the short term but can have serious consequences if continued over time. Carving off another slice of cheesecake or skipping class to sleep in may give you some immediate sense of pleasure, but one way or another, they often seem to degrade into feelings of regret. Spending Benjamins is just the same. You're in control—don't let money betray you. Figure 4 displays what people report as the most common subjects of buyer's remorse, as found in a study by the University of Cambridge—be wary when clothes shopping.

What to Do If You're Having Trouble Getting Started

Just do it.

Okay, in all seriousness, you get that this stuff is important, but phew, it seems like a lot of work to get everything set up. "Can't I just take a break and finish bingeing my show on Netflix?" you ask. No, we're going to do this now.

Follow these three steps to set up your emergency fund:

1. **Calculate your emergency fund goal** using a spread-sheet or piece of paper, summing up the living expenses in your budget.

2. **Pick a bank** to store your money, either a separately labeled bucket in your savings account at your existing bank, or set up a brand-new account somewhere else just for this purpose. As of this writing, banks that allow you to categorize your money in this way include Wealthfront, Ally, and Betterment (banks frequently offer cash incentives to new customers for opening checking or savings accounts, which a quick online search will prove). Keep yourself honest—if you know you are going to struggle to keep your hands out of the emergency pot, DO NOT house the money in the same account you use for everyday purchases. If your credit card and emergency fund ever get into a fight, the card will win every single time.

3. **Click transfer.** If you already have enough cash to set aside for your dedicated emergency fund, go ahead and transfer it in. If you only have part of it, transfer in what you can and update your budget to include an emergency fund contribution in the expenses list and contribute a chunk of your paycheck every month until you hit the target. If your emergency fund is set up in a different account than the one that your paycheck is deposited into, consider setting up an automatic, recurring transfer to shuffle the contribution in for you. The more frictionless you make your savings habits, the more likely you are to stick to them.

Congrats, you have just completed a huge step toward obtaining a more secure money situation. To put it profoundly, "That's one small click for you, one giant leap for your financial future." I'm thinking that after this chapter, you deserve a Netflix break.

"You Can't Touch This"

Did MC Hammer ever imagine that his infamous mantra would one day end up in a book teaching young adults how to build their first emergency fund? Doubtful. Well, thanks Hammer, because, quite literally, the money stashed away inside an emergency fund cannot be touched. *Except in the case of an emergency.* See? You know the words.

What scenarios actually constitute as a valid emergency will differ from person to person. For a working parent with a family of four to feed, losing a job would be an emergency—tap the account. For a pet lover whose sick dog desperately needs a trip to the veterinarian—tap the account. For a frequent commuter involved in an unfortunate wreck, with vehicle insurance requiring a $1,000 deductible—tap the account.

As you can see, the potential situations in which you may one day need to tap into your emergency fund can vary widely, but as a general rule of thumb it should only be used for essential expenses. It will be helpful for you to take some time to list out what could conceivably happen in your life that would be okay to deploy the emergency fund for. (I know it is unpleasant to think about these events, but it's good to be prepared just in case.) List what qualify as your emergencies in the worksheet at the end of this chapter.

An emergency fund turns a crisis into an inconvenience.

—Dave Ramsey, radio show host and personal finance advisor

Once you have that full month of living expenses in the bank, it's time to move to the next step. Later on, you will want to beef up your emergency fund even more, and I'll get to that, but first you should consider the benefits of putting your extra money toward the most reliable and profitable investment decision you can make—taking free cash from your employer.

Key Takeaways

- Your first emergency fund should equal one month of living expenses or $1,000, whichever is greater.
- Store your emergency fund in a separate account from the one you pay your typical expenses with; make it easily accessible, but not so easy that you are tempted to tap into it to make a frivolous purchase.
- Evaluate your own relationship with money. Do you feel that you could save more by shifting your spending mindset?

Take Action: Emergency Fund Worksheet

Using your budget, add up your monthly expenses. This number, or $1,000, will be your target emergency fund amount, whichever is greater. Then, think of the scenarios that could warrant using the funds and list them here.

EXAMPLE

Target Emergency Fund Amount: $2,850
I will only use it for true emergencies, such as when:

1. I lose my job
2. My car needs repairs
3. Rent increases unexpectedly
4. I become sick and cannot work
5. I get hit with an unexpected tax bill
6. My pet dog has an emergency
7. I have unexpected home repairs
8. A natural disaster strikes and I need to evacuate
9. I have to deal with a legal issue
10. A loved one gets ill

Target Emergency Fund Amount: _____
I will only use it for true emergencies, such as when:

1. _____
2. _____
3. _____
4. _____
5. _____
6. _____
7. _____
8. _____
9. _____
10. _____

Want a free printable copy of this worksheet?
Visit investnowplaylater.com/worksheets

Chapter 3

Max Out Your Employer-Matched Savings Plan

I f you don't really know what 401(k) stands for but you have a hunch it must mean when you have $401,000 in your bank account, well, you are wrong, but you are not alone—my sister spent all her college years under the exact same impression (which absolutely cracks me up).

But don't get me wrong. I can see the cause of confusion. Our wonderful lawmakers were not too creative when rolling out the 401(k) in 1978. Instead, they should have named it the "We'll Tax You Less If You Save for Your Retirement" account. That would have been clearer, and possibly would have encouraged more Americans to take advantage of it.

The 401(k) was brought to life in the United States with the passing of the Revenue Act of 1978, where section 401(k) of the document laid out the foundation for an employer-sponsored savings plan. Over time, this evolved into the modern account meant for retirement savings and investments with tax incentives for adding money to it. You can contribute up to a certain amount of your earnings to it each year, invest it, and then begin taking money out at retirement, beginning around age sixty.

If not already, you may find yourself working for a company that offers its employees a 401(k) retirement plan in the near future. And here is the best part—many employers want to encourage their employees to save (more savings = better financial security = less stress = happier employees), so they offer a match. For example, your employer may tell you that if you allow them to put aside 3% of your paycheck for your 401(k), they will then match 3% on top of your contribution, making it 6% total that is being deposited into the account. This free money is a huge deal, and I'll cover why.

Return on Investment

When someone talks about their return on investment, what exactly do they mean?

Let's break it down. When you invest your money, you are placing it somewhere you think it will grow, multiply itself, and be put to good use. And just how much money do you expect to get back in return? Well, that is measured by return on investment (ROI), which is the quantification of how good your investment turned out to be, often represented as a percentage. For example, if you decide to bake, decorate, and sell cookies as a side hustle, and you profit $300 in one month but had to invest $500 in a new mixer to get started, then your ROI on the mixer would be calculated like this:

(Profit from investment) / (Cost of investment) =
$300 / $500 = **60% return on investment**

As another example, say you are considering starting up a lawn care route on weekends but you need to purchase a $500 push lawn mower first so that you can cut grass. Figuring the route would bring in $750 a month, you would then need to subtract the cost of the lawn mower (plus fuel) to get your profit. We can assume that your monthly profit is $200. When we plug that into the ROI equation, we see that:

$$(\text{Profit from investment}) / (\text{Cost of investment}) =$$
$$\$200 / \$500 = \textbf{40\% return on investment}$$

These examples are very simplified, but as you can see, to get the most bang for your buck, you would choose to spend $500 on a mixer to start a baking business rather than $500 on a new lawn mower. A 60% ROI is better than a 40% ROI. You can seek ways to make your money grow quickest by comparing the ROI for each possible way it can be put to use.

This chapter is not about ROI or starting a business, but it's a good concept to grasp as you enter the world of investing. In particular, as you start out on your working career, you'll quickly realize that it is hard to beat the ROI of putting your money into your employer's 401(k) plan—particularly if they offer to match your contributions.

Contributing to a 401(k)

If your employer offers to match your 401(k) contributions, it's a no-brainer to take them up on it—just take a look at the ROI of that scenario. If, for example, your employer tells you that if you allow them to put aside 3% from each of your paychecks for your 401(k), they will then match 3% on top, you can plug this into a modified form of the ROI equation. Assuming you earn a $50,000 salary per year, you would have $125 taken from your paycheck each month:

(Profit from decision) / (Cost of decision) = $125 / $125 =
100% return on investment

The immediate $125 profit from your decision (as contributed to your account via your employer's match) provides you a remarkable 100% ROI. It is essentially free money. For this reason, many experts in personal finance recommend you do everything you can to take advantage of employer matches.

Once your budget is made, you have a small emergency fund, and you can afford the monthly bills for your necessities, focus all your spare cash toward contributing the minimum amount needed to get the maximum employer match in your 401(k) account.

If you are already meeting this goal, or if you will soon start, and you know you are able to contribute even more than what is required to get the minimum match, you have some decisions to make. There are pros and cons to going above and beyond with your 401(k) contributions.

Clearly, saving more is never a bad thing, however, your money could potentially have a greater ROI if you direct it elsewhere, as we'll explore in the rest of this book. So for the time being, if your employer offers a savings account with an employer match, contribute the amount needed to get the full employer match but nothing above that amount.

How Employer Matches Are Structured

Unfortunately, many employers are not the best at clearly communicating how a 401(k) match will work. For example, check out this gibberish that I took directly from one company's HR website: "Defined contribution is 2% minimum employer contribution +50% match on first 6% optional employee contribution above a 3% minimum employee contribution (i.e., 5% employer maximum, 14% total maximum)."

I mean, come on, what a mouthful that is. Here are some common match programs, broken down and simplified, for you to practice getting used to them. This might even help you better navigate future job offers. (Yes, you should always ask your employer whether they offer a savings plan match if you are based in the US.)

Employer A

- **Offer:** "Defined contribution is 2% minimum employer contribution +50% match on first 6% optional employee contribution above a 3% minimum employee contribution (i.e., 5% employer maximum, 14% total maximum)."
- **Translation:** The employer will automatically contribute 2% of your salary into your 401(k) as free money. They will give you even more free money if you choose to save at least 3%—any amount you save between 3% and 6%, the employer will match half of it (for example, if you choose to save 5%, the company will give you 4.5% of your salary in free money).

Employer B

- **Offer:** "Contribute a minimum of 6% of your pay to the Savings Plan by payroll deduction. This is called your minimum contribution. The company matches only your minimum contribution with 7% of your pay."
- **Translation:** The employer will automatically contribute 7% of your salary into your 401(k) as free money if you save at least 6% of your salary.

Employer C

- **Offer:** "For every $1 of employee contribution you make (up to 4% of your eligible pay), we will contribute $0.50 to your account in the form of matching contributions. You can get up to a 2% match."
- **Translation:** The employer will automatically match half of what you save in your 401(k), up to 2% maximum. To get the most free money possible, you need to save 4% of your salary.

Employers A, B, and C all want to incentivize their employees to pursue financial fitness by contributing to their 401(k) account, but they go about it in different ways. As you go through your career, you'll notice that some employers provide a set percentage match, usually half, of their employees' contributions up to a certain maximum (that would be Employers A and C), while some may reward you with a flat contribution of their own as soon as you save a certain amount (like Employer B).

For the majority of 401(k) programs, the money you elect to contribute will be taken directly out of your paycheck. So as long as you have budgeted for it, it's almost like a set-it-and-forget-it type situation.

And on your pay stub, which typically breaks down how much of your earnings are being deducted for taxes, insurance premiums, and other costs, you will also see a line for the 401(k) contribution from YOUR earnings as well as a contribution from your EMPLOYER's side (which does not affect your take-home pay, because it's free money).

Now, you should always be skeptical when someone offers you free money. "What's the catch?" you may ask.

Here's the thing: most companies that offer a 401(k) match will mention vesting in the fine print. Vesting is a way to encourage workers to stick around. As an employee, you are vested once you have worked for your employer for a specified number of years, at which point the contribution of the employer will become fully yours.

For example, a three-year vesting schedule is probably what you'll see most often—with this agreement, you will only be able to keep the free money that your employer contributed to your 401(k) account if you work for them for at least three years. If you leave the company before reaching three years of service, you will still have money you contributed from your paycheck (don't worry, that isn't forfeited), but the dollars that came from your employer match will be returned to the company.

After you are fully vested, however, you own 100% of the account balance, and your employer cannot take it back for any reason. The bottom line is to make sure you understand your employer's vesting schedule before you decide to switch jobs.

If you need any more convincing that you should do everything in your power to take advantage of employer matches, take a look at how a small difference in how Jacob and Emily managed their money impacted their future wealth.

Both Jacob and Emily work for an employer that offers to match half of what they contribute, up to a maximum of 3% of their salary.

Both earn $50,000 per year and started investing in their 401(k) plans at age twenty-five. Jacob elects to contribute 3% of his salary to the plan, thus getting an additional 1.5% match from the employer. Emily, on the other hand, contributes 6% of her salary and thus gets the maximum 3% match. Both accounts compound at 9.7% annually.

At retirement, Emily will have $1,107,000 more than Jacob. Figure 5 will help you visualize this outcome.

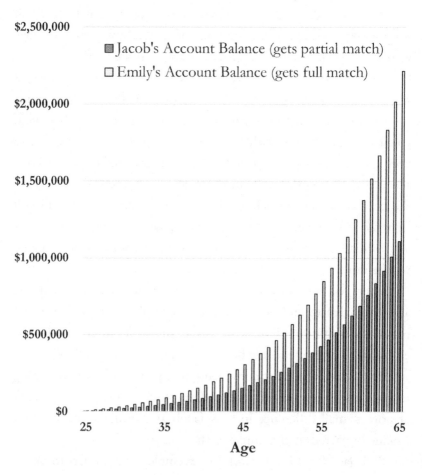

Figure 5: The Impact of Maxing Out Your Employer Match over Time

As of this writing, nearly 70% of Americans have access to an employer-sponsored 401(k) plan, but only 41% contribute to one, per the US Census Bureau. This is a disheartening fact, and not only because of all the wasted free money these people are leaving on the table, but also because they are missing out on a super powerful way to grow money through investing their 401(k) in the stock market.

I discussed the magic of compounding earlier, and I mentioned how the stock market can give you phenomenal returns over time, but I didn't cover how the stock market operates. As a young person, it is a great idea to use the money in your 401(k) account to buy stocks, and here's how it works.

The Stock Market and Your 401(k)

Just as you might require money to get a degree or certification in your field and build your future, corporations require money (aka capital) to build their businesses. To raise this capital, they sell fractions of themselves to the public—shares of stock. A share of stock represents a piece of the pie of a whole company, and the stock market is a venue for trading these shares. Well-known stock markets include the New York Stock Exchange (NYSE), National Association of Securities Dealers Automated Quotations (Nasdaq), and London Stock Exchange (LSE).

To buy a portion, or share, of a company, there must be another person on the other side of the transaction to sell it to you. Likewise, to sell a share of stock, someone must be willing to buy it. When there are more buyers than sellers, the stock price rises—the simple law of supply and demand. People are willing to pay more and more for ownership of the company (usually because they believe that it will increase in value). And vice versa—when there are more sellers than buyers, the stock price drops.

Hundreds of millions of shares of stock are traded every day. Well, every Monday through Friday, excluding federal holidays, of course.

Now, there are two primary ways that being a shareholder (stock owner) can pay off:

1. An increase in the price of the stock
2. Income generated by dividend payments

As the value of a company rises, the price of the stock you own increases, and at some point, you will (hopefully) be able to sell your shares for more money than you paid to purchase them.

Dividend payments are a little more involved. A dividend is a corporation's payment to shareholders just for existing. Dividend payments are quarterly payouts (every three months) of a company's earnings, deposited straight into your account. And the more shares you hold, the more dividends you will receive. Larger, more stable corporations are the most frequent issuers of dividend payments, and they often increase their dividend payments annually.

As an example, say you own 100 shares of The Coca-Cola Company. As of this writing, the quarterly shareholder dividend payment is $0.44 per share. How much will you get paid, just for owning 100 shares of Coca-Cola stock?

$0.44 per share x 100 shares = $44 per dividend payment
$44 per payment x 4 payments per year = $176 per year

$176 per year, just for owning shares in the company. Easy money, right? It gets even better though. Remember, you also make money if the price of each share increases, as shown in Figure 6. If you bought 100 shares of Coca-Cola stock on December 31, 2009, you would have paid around $19.07 per share, for a total of $1,907. Thirteen years later, on December 31, 2022, your initial investment would now be worth $6,291, considering both the increase in share price and reinvested dividend payouts—an annual return of 9.6%.

You read that right. You can automatically reinvest your dividend payments to buy more shares and therefore receive even more dividend payments (this is a very common thing and is easy to do—more on this later). Compounding at work!

Figure 6: Coca-Cola Stock Performance, Including Dividend Reinvestment

Now, to be clear, the stock market is not always this rosy. There is risk involved with all investments, and out of all the available types, stocks are considered on the riskier side. You could technically lose all your invested money if a company goes bankrupt, and many past investors have.

Still, there are ways to mitigate this risk. It is actually encouraged to have a healthy amount of risk in your investments—especially for investors on the younger side—because as your risk increases, your potential reward increases as well.

Most experts recommend that people have an investment strategy that naturally reduces risk when approaching retirement by spreading out their collection of investments across stocks, bonds, annuities, real estate investment trusts (REITs), and other investments. This is called diversification. However, I am ignoring bonds, annuities, and REITs in this book because the approaches here are designed for someone in the early years of their life.

A young person can ride the ups and downs of the stock market easier than someone five years from retirement. For young investors, taking on the extra risk now will likely result in greater rewards in the long run. This is referred to as taking on a more aggressive investment strategy, and it will likely suit your 401(k) well.

Further to this point, diversification will allow you to spread out your risk. You have likely heard the phrase "don't put all your eggs in one basket." If your entire investment account consists of one stock, and it drops and goes bankrupt, your money is gone. Instead, try to invest in a variety of companies in a variety of industries. The collection of companies you own is called your portfolio. Hopefully, your portfolio will have more winners than losers.

To recap the key stock market takeaways:

1. When you buy a share of stock, you become partial owner of that company—you are invested in its future.
2. Owning stock can make you money in two ways: an increase in share price and dividend payments.

You may be thinking, "Well this is fine and dandy, but I still don't know how to pick the right stock." That's okay, because you will likely not be picking most of your portfolio yourself. Study after study has shown that you will do much better by investing in a preallocated, diversified portfolio of companies that track the overall market. Sound boring? Maybe. Unfortunately, lots of money management is boring. But I think your future self will thank you for learning this all now and actioning it while you're young.

To get the best shot at making money in the stock market without too much risk, most professionals recommend investing your money into one fund that aggregates the prices of many different stocks and puts them all into one basket. These are called exchange-traded funds (ETFs)—you may have heard of them.

ETFs are an excellent way to invest in the stock market. A common ETF is VOO, which is a Vanguard fund that tracks the S&P 500 index, the five hundred largest companies in America. On average, over time, the S&P 500 has gone up 9.7% per year (though not without its bumps along the way; 9.7% is just an average). Soon, we'll discuss what steps to take to ensure that your 401(k) is invested in this manner.

Many investors try to beat the performance of the S&P 500 by picking and choosing individual stocks to buy and sell at random points throughout the year. Unfortunately, the vast majority of these investors fail. They may have big winners every once in a while, but to consistently outperform the entire market is no easy feat. For that reason, the compounded returns of the S&P 500 are just fine for me. Yes, buying boring old ETFs can make you a millionaire.

> *Don't look for the needle in the haystack.*
> *Just buy the haystack!*

> — John Bogle, creator of the index fund

Before I wrap up talking about stocks, there is one more thing to touch on: taxes. Or the lack thereof. Up to this point in your life, you have not had to think about taxes very much. If only that could continue.

When you sell stocks for a profit, you incur a capital gains tax, which is collected by the government. However, there is a way to avoid losing your hard-invested dollars to taxes if you save and invest through the correct account type—the 401(k) being one of them.

Traditional vs. Roth 401(k)s

When you sign up for a 401(k) plan, chances are your employer will give you the option to do a traditional 401(k) or a Roth 401(k). If they give you no option (or just call it a 401(k), plain and simple), then it is a traditional plan. I know what you're likely thinking—"Just another confusing layer, why is this so complicated?" Again, my apologies on behalf of our lawmakers for the complexity of this system. I will do my best to simplify the two account types for you now.

Saving and investing for retirement inside of a 401(k) plan isn't only great because of the match that your employer may provide—it's also a very tax efficient way to grow money. Money that you invest inside of any old brokerage account (think Robinhood or E*TRADE or Fidelity) will be taxed twice. TWICE!

That's right, Uncle Sam is hungry for tax revenue and your (1) income taxes and (2) capital gains taxes will help feed his appetite. Inside a traditional or Roth 401(k), however, you should only be taxed once. Traditional 401(k)s are taxed when you retire, while Roth 401(k)s are taxed when you originally earn the income.

Bear with me here. I'm going to break it down with a bit of math and then highlight which account type is best. To do this, let's travel the path of a hypothetical $10,000 from your yearly salary, depending on which of these three account types you decide to use:

- **Taxable Brokerage Account:** Your $10,000 is taxed as income when you earn it, with an estimated ~$1,650 going toward income taxes (typically deducted from your paycheck); you are left with $8,350, which you invest in an S&P 500 ETF like VOO; it compounds at 9.7% per year and in forty years it is worth $340,000. Awesome, but you have to pay taxes again on your capital gains. Poof, there goes ~$56,000, **leaving you with $284,000 (taxed twice)**.
- **Traditional 401(k) Account:** Your $10,000 contribution is tax deductible the year you contribute it, meaning you

are able to put the whole amount into your account before paying any taxes on it. There, it grows at 9.7% per year until forty years later, when it is worth $406,000; however, now you have to pay taxes on it, reducing the sum by about $70,000 and **leaving you with $336,000 (taxed once, at retirement).**

- **Roth 401(k) Account:** Your $10,000 has to be contributed *after* paying income taxes on it, so for the purposes of this example, we can assume you start with $8,350. As in the brokerage account example, it grows to $340,000 and, fortunately, you don't have to pay any more taxes on it. **Leaving you with $340,000 (taxed once, at original paycheck).**

So which account is the winner? Clearly, getting your hard-earned dollars taxed once is better than getting them taxed twice, so having either type of 401(k) will always beat out a regular taxable brokerage account. But between the traditional and Roth 401(k), the latter will usually be the winner for young adults. Why?

Well, when you take money out of a traditional 401(k) at retirement, you must pay taxes on the money based on your tax bracket *at that time*. Typically, once you go through thirty to forty years of a career, you can expect to be getting paid substantially more than you are now, and thus you'll likely be in a higher tax bracket.

The younger you start saving and investing for retirement, the more enticing the Roth account becomes. This is why setting up a Roth 401(k) may be in your best interest. Table 3 shows when you are typically taxed based on the account type you have.

Table 3: Taxable Events by Account Type

	Roth 401(k)	Traditional 401(k)	Taxable Brokerage Account
Earn Money	Taxable Event		Taxable Event
Investment Goes Up in Value			
Selling for a Profit			Taxable Event
Receive Dividend Payments			Taxable Event
When You Withdraw		Taxable Event	

Note that these examples assumed a salary of today of $50,000 and a salary at retirement age of $83,000, in alignment with current US averages. Salary at retirement is an important metric in the evaluation of a traditional 401(k) account, because the higher your salary, the higher tax rate you'll need to pay when you withdraw money from your account.

If you aren't located in the United States, the particulars of the 401(k) clearly do not apply to you. However, many countries have instituted similar savings incentives for their citizens that would be worth researching.

The 403(b), 457(b), TSP, and Solo 401(k)

More tax codes and acronyms—yay. In addition to the previously discussed plans, there are a few other options you should be aware of in case your current employer, or a future one, does not offer the standard 401(k) selections.

I won't dive into the details on these, but just know that they are worth looking into depending on your situation, and they all have tax incentives similar to a traditional 401(k).

- A **403(b)** is a retirement plan for certain employees of public schools, employees of certain tax-exempt organizations, and certain ministers. A 403(b) plan allows employees to contribute some of their salary to the plan.
- **457(b)** plans are generally available for state and local government employees, as well as certain tax-exempt nonprofits.
- A **thrift savings plan (TSP)** is a retirement investment program open only to federal employees and members of the armed services.
- A **solo 401(k)** is an individual 401(k) designed for a business owner with no employees.

As you can see, government employees and people working for tax-exempt institutions are generally offered one of these plans for retirement savings. Their specific tax treatment, maximum contributions, and more information can be found at **www.irs.gov**.

The Money Is in the Account—Now What?

You may be inclined to think that once you've told your employer what percentage of your paycheck you'd like to stash away in your new 401(k), you're in the clear and finally done.

Sometimes you truly are finished at this point, and sometimes you aren't.

One of the most confusing concepts for new investors is the notion that you need to make sure that the money you contribute to an investment account is actually being invested instead of just sitting there as cash. Cash goes down in value. Investments go up in value. You want to make sure your money is actually invested so that it can grow.

Unfortunately, the problem of whether your money is automatically invested varies widely from person to person because it is highly dependent on how your employer's 401(k) system is set up and which plan provider they have partnered with (common 401(k) providers include T. Rowe Price, Fidelity, Charles Schwab, Merrill Edge, ADP, and Voya Financial).

The majority of these providers will ask you how you would like your contributions to be allocated when you sign up for the plan, and they will automatically take the cash you contribute from each paycheck (plus the match dollars your employer throws in) and use those funds to buy your preselected investment options. Then you can just sit back and watch your account balance grow.

Other providers, however, will require you to manually login to your account and "purchase" investments with your money once it is transferred in from your paycheck. It cannot be overstated how crucial it is for you to make sure that your money is being invested inside of your 401(k) and not just sitting inside as cash.

Ask your manager, peers at work, or HR contact to address any questions while you are setting up the account or checking in on an existing one—there's no shame in making sure your money is working for you as hard as it should be.

Choosing What to Invest In

Very few employer-sponsored 401(k) plans will allow you to invest in individual stocks. Instead, they offer diverse baskets of stocks all wrapped up into one fund. There are thousands of funds available in the financial markets, but your company's 401(k) plan will only offer a small selection of stock and bond funds, ranging from conservative to more aggressive. And this is for good reason, because your provider will charge far less in transaction fees when the investment options are limited, which means more money for you later.

A common exception to this, however, is when the company you work for is publicly traded on the stock market and wants to allow you the ability—and even encourage you sometimes by offering discounts—to purchase its own shares as an investment.

Recall, however, that it is a common recommendation among professionals that you keep the majority of your long-term investment dollars in funds (such as ETFs) that buy shares of many different companies. Your 401(k) plan may not allow you to buy a share of stock in Coca-Cola (KO), but it most certainly allows you to access KO through its fund that tracks the S&P 500. When you invest in a fund that includes the S&P 500, you are investing in those five hundred top companies all at once. Congratulations, business owner.

When you are first setting up your 401(k) account, either traditional or Roth, you are likely to be asked what funds you would like everything allocated to: In other words, how do you want your money to be invested? In general, you'll be presented with an option for cash or money market, bonds, international stocks, and US stocks.

Money market and bond funds can almost be completely disregarded as a young investor. Historically, the best returns have come from investing long term in stocks. The money market/cash and bond offerings are typically geared toward someone closing in on retirement (because those two options are less risky; once you make your money, you don't want to lose it).

Many professionals will recommend that you split your investments between two funds—roughly 75% in US stocks and 25% in international stocks. Back testing has proven this to be a consistent allocation sweet spot.

In my own 401(k) plan, my employer offers the following options:

- Equity Units—S&P 500 Composite Stock Price Index (five hundred largest US companies)
- Extended Market Units—Dow Jones US Completion Total Stock Market Index (all US stocks not included in the S&P 500)
- International Equity Units—MSCI World excluding US Investable Market Index (an index fund that invests in about 3,700 international companies in twenty-three developed countries outside the US)
- Bond Units—Barclays US Aggregate Bond Index (about eight thousand investment-grade US-based bonds)
- Balanced Fund Units—includes all of the proceeding four index funds, rebalanced monthly so that your money is their recommended 35% Equity/15% Extended Market/25% International Equity/25% Bond
- Common Assets—short- and medium-term fixed-income fund (basically a cash account earning interest just like your savings at a bank)

Whether or not your 401(k) provider offers more, fewer, or the same investment funds as mine, you'll need to do a bit of research before you make your selections.

One of my favorite ways to assess each fund you're offered is to search its name via Morningstar, an investment research firm. On Morningstar's site, you'll be taken to a profile page for the fund, which will list its fees, performance over time, and what companies, sectors, stocks, and bonds make up the fund. Morningstar also provides a star rating for each investment's performance.

If you're craving even more info, you can always search the fund's name on Google too. It's pretty quick to find what companies comprise the fund, what its goal is (growth/aggressive funds = higher risk while fixed-income funds = lower risk) and more.

Be careful when doing your research though. You definitely don't want to just look at a fund's performance from last year and make an investment decision based on that. Instead, take it back more long term. Five- and ten-year returns will give you a better idea of how the fund has performed over time.

Beware of Fees

And yes, of course, these funds all do charge fees, which it would be wise of you to pay attention to. Fees, most often called the expense ratio, are automatically deducted from the displayed value of your investment within your account. This is convenient but it makes it difficult to realize the money you might be giving away if you own a fund with a particularly high expense ratio.

Target for a fee below 1% in any mutual fund or ETF you invest in. As of this writing, Vanguard's S&P 500 ETF fund, VOO, only charges 0.03%. That means for every $1,000 you have invested, you pay only $0.30 in fees per year. That's a steal.

As of this writing, the average expense ratio of all ETFs is 0.44% but can range as low as 0.03% and as high as 1.0%. A 0.44% expense ratio would mean that owning the fund would cost you $4.40 in fees for every $1,000 that you have invested into it, each year. Compounded over time, these fees get very pricey and can take a sizable chunk out of your retirement fund.

Just take a quick comparison of Michael's 401(k) balance at retirement versus Madison's. Both people earned $50,000 per year for their entire careers, contributed 6% of their salary to their 401(k) plans beginning at age twenty-five, received an employer match of 3%, and enjoyed compounded returns matching the US stock market, about 9.7% annually.

However, Michael chose to invest his funds in a low-cost ETF with a 0.05% expense ratio, while Madison unknowingly opted for a fund with a 1% expense ratio. As shown in Figure 7, at retirement, Michael will have $519,680 more than Madison.

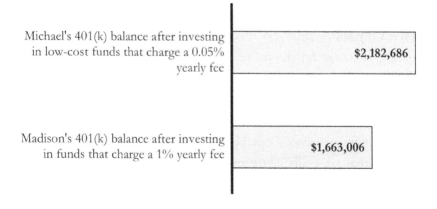

Figure 7: The Impact of Fees on Your 401(k) Balance at Retirement

Your 401(k) plan may offer mutual funds in addition to ETFs. Most mutual funds are typically more actively managed, so the fees are higher. The managers are constantly swapping out shares of one company for another, to beat the market. However, on average, over time, many mutual funds usually do not beat the broader market indexes, but the fees they charge sure make it seem like they do.

Please do not get me wrong—some mutual funds put out returns that make the management fees worth it, but you must be careful. The average expense ratio of a mutual fund as of this writing is around 0.79% but can range from 0.5% to 2.5%. Some mutual funds also charge a one-time fee when you buy into it (called the load), but there are many no-load options available as well.

As alluded to, unfortunately, the magic of compounding applies to fees as well, and the magnifying effect is incredible. For example, a 1% annual expense ratio on a $10,000 investment can reduce your total returns by almost 17% after twenty years of compounding. This gap widens even further as you increase the time frame. Ignoring fees when picking investments is a huge mistake.

While we're on the topic of fees, it's worth bringing up financial advisors. You may have one already, or are considering getting one. Here's my take—financial advisors are terrific for people who either have absolutely no desire, or just lack the discipline, to manage their own finances.

Any person would be much better off paying someone to invest for them rather than not invest at all. In this case, paying fees to hire a financial advisor can be well worth it in the long run. The issue is that it's really not that complicated to DIY when you are young. Chances are, you don't have any complicated tax strategies or estate planning to do. Instead, just pile your money into low-fee ETFs, set up recurring contributions, and sit back and wait.

As Personal Finance Club's Jeremy Schneider puts it, it may be time to "break up" with your financial advisor. A financial advisor who charges just a 1% annual advisory fee and recommends actively managed mutual funds that charge (an additional) 1% expense ratio, that 2% net fee will erode about half of your portfolio over a forty-year investing career—losing $950,000 for the average American and lining the pockets of advisors and fund managers instead.

People investing less than $250K will not receive as favorable terms. Advisors who work with such individuals may impose front loads, statement fees, and other charges, which could significantly reduce gains.

Therefore, during the wealth-building phase of your life, minimizing fees is one of the few actionable steps that can be taken to maximize returns.

If you currently hire a financial advisor and want to leave them, consider opening an account separate from them and putting $1,000 or so into it, practice investing the money until you get the hang of it, and then send your advisor an email telling them you want to move on and want to self-manage your money. Then, initiate a transfer of the assets from your advisor by telling your new brokerage account to pull them in and set up your new investments. It's that easy.

If there's one DIY project in your life that's worth it, learning how to manage your own money is it, to the tune of nearly a million dollars.

Target-Date Funds

If you are feeling a bit overwhelmed by all these nuances, don't fret. First off, you're not alone. Second, there's a way you can invest that takes all of this advice and wraps it into one tidy package that is automatically updated for you as you progress through life.

More and more plans are allowing savers to opt for a target-date fund, which takes most of the guesswork out of the equation. With these funds, you select a target retirement year and risk tolerance, and the fund is automatically set to an appropriate asset allocation for you.

These are options for beginner investors who don't want to be very hands-on in managing their money. The great thing about target-date funds is that they do all the hard work for you, like making sure your money is invested in different kinds of assets so that you don't lose all your money if one thing doesn't do well. They also make sure your money becomes less risky as you get closer to retiring so you don't lose it all right when you need it.

"Most people aren't interested in researching [and] selecting funds for their 401(k)," said Charles C. Weeks, a Philadelphia-based CFP (certified financial planner), in an interview with CNBC. "Target date funds will help people avoid blowing up their portfolios by making avoidable mistakes like putting too much in one asset class, chasing returns by investing based on past performance and/or letting greed and fear dictate their investment strategy."

Target-date index funds are offered by most of the major brokers. If you're going to invest with this set-it-and-permanently-forget-it method, you will need to choose one based on your age. As a general rule of thumb, take the year you were born and add 65 to it. Then, choose the ticker symbol for the closest year. For example, someone born in 1997 with a Vanguard account would choose VTTSX, as per below:

$$1997 + 65 = 2062$$

Target-date funds are typically only offered in five-year increments, so rounding is necessary in this example. The closest offering to a 2062 retirement year is the 2060 fund, as shown in Table 4.

Table 4: Target-Date Index Fund Offerings by Broker

Approx. Retirement Year	Vanguard	Fidelity	Charles Schwab
2040	VFORX	FBIFX	SWYGX
2045	VTIVX	FIOFX	SWYHX
2050	VFIFX	FIPFX	SWYMX
2055	VFFVX	FDEWX	SWYJX
2060	VTTSX	FDKLX	SWYNX
2065	VLXVX	FFSFX	SWYOX

Over time, the fund will automatically rebalance, becoming more conservative as you near retirement, as represented in Figure 8. If you choose a target-date fund, you only need to choose the one fund—otherwise, you're essentially canceling out its benefits by throwing your risk profile out of whack. If you find that you want to be a bit on the riskier side, you can select a date farther in the future, or sooner if you desire less risk.

Are target-date funds worth doing? At the end of the day, target-date funds are more conservative and diversified, but have long-term underperformance and slightly higher fees than a regular old S&P 500 index fund. But if you cruise into retirement in forty years with 100% of your money in an S&P 500 index fund, you (while having a lot of money) are also going to have a lot of volatility from day to day.

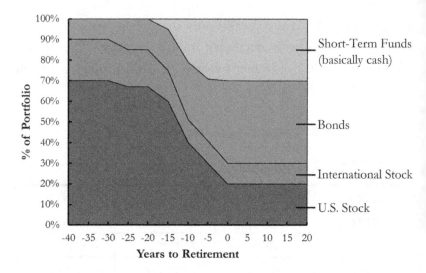

Figure 8: Typical Target-Date Fund Glide Path

It's really far in the future, but as you approach retirement, you'll need to sell off stocks in exchange for bonds and cash—this is called rebalancing. If you don't trust yourself to remember to do that, it may be worth going for the target-date fund that will sacrifice some total returns, but you'll definitely be much better off than not investing in either.

Match and Move On

At this stage in your personal finance journey, most experts recommend contributing just enough to your 401(k) to enable you to get the maximum amount of free match money from your employer, but no more. Of course, the IRS will allow you to contribute quite a bit more than this (up to $22,500 annually as of this writing), but there could quite possibly be better uses for your excess money, which I'll walk you through in the subsequent chapters.

Eventually, when you're a sharp-shooting budgeter, resolute saver, and debt-wrangling money whiz, you'll want to revisit your 401(k) and contribute more to make sure you're saving enough for retirement.

If your employer doesn't offer to match any of your 401(k) plan contributions, should you still add money to the account? The short answer is yes, because the tax advantages still exist. Also, keep in mind that contributing to a 401(k) is a form of forced savings, which can be helpful if you have trouble saving money on your own. However, if you find yourself in a situation without a match, consider taking action to eliminate debt (chapter 4) and max out a Roth IRA (chapter 5) prior to looping back to the opportunity to contribute to your 401(k).

Investing money automatically from each paycheck for retirement is a great idea, and when your employer throws you free money to do so, it's a no-brainer.

Now that this step has been addressed, it is time to turn our attention back to the spending side of things. Or rather, over-spending with money you don't have. Chapter 4 will walk through the pay down of high-interest debts so that you can free yourself for the later strategies that will really build your wealth.

Key Takeaways

- If you are lucky enough to work for an employer with a savings plan, take advantage of their automatic match. It's an immediate 100% return on your investment.

- Money in your 401(k) account can be invested in the stock market, which has, on average, compounded 9.7% annually.
- Contributing part of your paycheck to a 401(k) plan will reduce your taxes, either now or when you take the money out, depending on the way you set it up.

Take Action: 401(k) Contribution Worksheet

If you aren't already maximizing your employer's 401(k) match, now is the time to run the numbers so that you can see how increasing your contributions will impact your monthly budget.

EXAMPLE

My employer will match up to **3.0**% of my salary.

To get the maximum match from my employer, they say that I must contribute at least **6.0**%.

My average monthly salary (before taxes) is **$4,167**.

To get the max match, the amount I need to contribute to my 401(k) each month is **6.0**% of **$4,167** = **$250**.

Now, you'll need to take this answer and incorporate it into your budget.

My employer will match up to _____% of my salary.

To get the maximum match from my employer, they say that I must contribute at least _____%.

My average monthly salary (before taxes) is $_____.

To get the max match, the amount I need to contribute to my 401(k) each month is _____% of $_____ = $_____.

Now, you'll need to take this answer and incorporate it into your budget.

1. Sum up your total monthly expenses.
2. Subtract the incremental 401(k) contribution per the calculations above.
3. Reevaluate your monthly expenses to determine if any changes need to be made to accommodate the new contribution amount.
4. Make necessary adjustments to your budget to ensure that you can reasonably contribute the necessary amount to your 401(k) to maximize your employer match.

Want a free printable copy of this worksheet?
Visit investnowplaylater.com/worksheets

Chapter 4

Pay Down High-Interest Debt

One in ten Americans has a negative net worth. Negative. What exactly does that mean?

Your net worth is negative when the value of what you *owe* is greater than the value of what you *own*. Without a doubt, a poll of people closer to the ages of young adults would register an even higher fraction of negative net worth individuals, particularly due to student debt.

When someone owes money to someone else, we call that being in debt. If you pay a monthly car loan, you are in debt. If you have a credit card balance, you are in debt, and if you have a mortgage on your house, you are in debt (yes, you own the house, but you are in debt to the bank who lent you money to purchase it). Once all these items that you owe are summed up and compared to the stuff you actually own, it isn't too difficult for things to get, well, negative.

When an individual experiences a negative net worth for a prolonged period of time, this is often an indicator of chronic financial hardship, and people operating within the constraints of debt have little room for error. They may be one job loss or unexpected expense away from having to declare bankruptcy. And the thing with debt is that, while it is certainly feasible to break free of most any situation with the correct plan, it becomes unquestionably more difficult to escape the deeper you fall into debt.

Recall from our earlier discussion on investment returns that there is a profound impact on growth due to compounding—the money you invest makes money, which makes more money and so on.

Well, you may be surprised to learn that the exact same principle can be applied to the majority of your debts. The money you owe is charged interest by your lender, which, if you don't pay it off quick enough, is added into the bucket of money you owe, and then you have to pay interest on your original owed money plus its prior interest charges. The money you owe causes you to owe more money, which causes you to owe more money. It's a downward spiral of indebtedness.

Figure 9 plots the trends in debt categories among people with a negative net worth according to a Federal Reserve Board Survey of Consumer Finances. Notice that student debt and credit cards are at the top of the list.

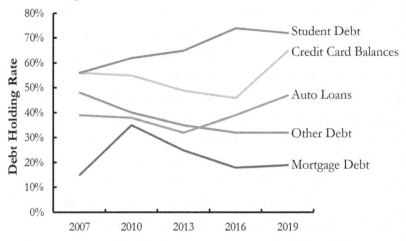

Figure 9: Debt Holding Rates among Negative Net Worth Households

Credit cards, for example, can charge as much as 24% APR (annual percentage rate) on balances as of this writing. If you thought 9.7% annual growth in the stock market could build your wealth fast, just imagine how quickly a 24% compounded debt could decimate you. To make matters worse, the majority of credit card issuers compound interest on a daily basis. This means that your interest is added to your principal (original) balance at the end of every day. If you put $1,000 worth of clothes on a 24% APR credit card and take five years to pay it off, you'll have spent a total of $1,726 on those clothes—nearly double.

High-interest debts such as credit cards, auto loans, and personal loans are the biggest threats to achieving your financial goals. If you have any debt with an interest rate (APR) of 10% or higher, you have come to the point in your personal financial checklist when you finally have to do something about it—no more procrastination.

Leaders in the area of debt elimination, such as Dave Ramsey, have provided us with well-researched strategies to tackle your debt problems. Two strategies in particular can best be grouped by the psychological strength required to enact them (and as we see yet again, personal finance is personal so you've got to choose your own way). Here is a quick breakdown of the avalanche and snowball debt reduction methods.

The Snowball Method

The snowball method is aptly named for its analogy of a snowball rolling down a hill. When the snowball starts out, it's relatively loose and fluffy, but after rolling for a bit, it gets more compact and begins to grow larger and larger, gaining momentum all the while.

You can apply this idea to your debt reduction plan, as well. First, sort your debts from lowest to highest amount owed (regardless of interest rate). Next, make the minimum monthly payments on all of your debts except for the smallest. Target all your excess money toward paying off this smallest balance first, then move down the list.

When you move to tackle the second lowest debt, for example, you should apply a payment worth the minimum payment of what used to be your first debt, plus the minimum payment of your current debt target, plus anything and everything extra you can put toward it each month. Repeat this for the third smallest debt, fourth smallest debt, and so on until you eliminate them all.

Because you are tackling the "easiest" jobs first, many people find the snowball method to be a great psychological approach to debt elimination. Your monthly debt-blasting snowball payment will keep getting larger and larger with each account that you pay off, and you'll likely find that your confidence in money management grows alongside it. You typically begin to see results very early in the process. If you are more confident in your willpower, however, you may be interested to learn that there is an approach that will save you time and money—the avalanche method.

The Avalanche Method

In the snowball method, you organize your debts from smallest to largest balance, but with the avalanche method, you sort them from highest to lowest interest rate and work down the list from there. The primary benefit of paying off the highest rate first is that you'll end up paying less in interest and fees overall. Similar to the snowball method, make minimum payments on the rest of the debts.

Another perk of this method is that you'll typically finish your debt reduction journey earlier than with the snowball method; after all, an avalanche moves down the side of a mountain quite quickly.

Note, however, that this approach requires the most discipline to pull off. Your highest interest rate debt may not necessarily be your smallest debt, so you may be stuck working on it for a while. And if your largest debt has the largest interest rate, it's going to be a long time before you start to see a dent in its balance. Even if it's difficult to see any progress, you cannot give up.

Table 5 compares the two methods side by side and shows how they could impact your total debt payments. Note that this is purely mathematical and assumes that both are equally difficult to follow through with psychologically.

Table 5: Comparing the Avalanche and Snowball Methods for Hypothetical Debts

	Avalanche Method	Snowball Method
First Debt to Pay Off	$10,000 credit card debt at 18.99%	$9,000 car loan at 3.00%
Second Debt to Pay Off	$15,000 student loan at 4.50%	$10,000 credit card debt at 18.99%
Third Debt to Pay Off	$9,000 car loan at 3.00%	$15,000 student loan at 4.50%
Total Time Required	~11 months	~11.2 months
Total Interest Paid	$1,012	$1,515

At the end of the day, which debt reduction method you choose will be dependent upon your personal situation and whether you feel confident in your ability to redirect a sizable portion of your budget toward paying off your debt. Another note: it is recommended that neither the avalanche or snowball method should be used for mortgages (loans used to purchase a house), so if you have one, exclude it from the list. The Debt Repayment Worksheet at the end of this chapter will assist you in making your own game plan.

Last, it's important to recognize that neither the snowball or the avalanche method will improve your financial situation if you continue adding to your debt, particularly credit card debt. Speaking of credit cards...

Your Credit Card Is Your Frenemy

One of the most commonly used forms of debt is the credit card. I like to consider credit cards my frenemy (enemy who pretends to be a friend) because they have lots of perks, but they can be weapons of mass financial destruction in the hands of the wrong people.

Credit cards are offered by big banks because the more you swipe, the more they profit. And yes, if credit cards are good at one thing, it's that they sure do make it easy for you to SPEND MONEY. As I've hit home repeatedly, overspending is no bueno when you're trying to get your financial life in order. Studies show that people spend an average of about 50% more when paying for fast food with a card versus with cash. Don't be one of those people.

Credit cards use money from the credit card company's bank account as soon as you swipe, tap, wave, or click *checkout*—so you don't pay for the item you purchased until you send money back to the credit card company when paying your monthly bill. But don't forget that this borrowed money isn't free. You have to pay extra on top of the initial amount that you spent (interest) if you don't pay your card's bill on time. If you have a credit card, always pay your bill by the statement due date so you don't end up paying interest and late fees.

Most credit cards give you the option to make a very low minimum payment every month instead of paying the entire amount you owe. This minimum payment may seem like a good deal, but beware, if you pay anything less than your full state-ment balance every month, your credit card company will start charging you interest. If you make only the minimum credit card payments on a new $400 suit, for example, you'll be paying around $15 each month. If you make these minimum payments until it is completely paid off (around three years later), that suit will have cost you a total of around $535.

Paying interest on a lot of credit card debt can start to feel like you're swimming against the current. You kick harder and harder, but you aren't going anywhere. Remember that if you are a borrower, like when using a credit card, you want interest rates to be as low as possible. In this example, the credit card used to make your suit purchase carries a typical interest rate of 19.99%.

If you have a credit card now (or plan to get one in the future), think twice before using it. You don't want to end up paying much more for something than it actually costs. Besides, you have options for making payments for things other than using credit cards.

There are apps that you can pay with, which you can set up to pull directly from your bank account. Payment apps like Venmo, PayPal, Zelle, and Cash App all allow you to quickly send and receive money to or from your friends and businesses.

Debit cards allow you to make purchases with the money in your checking account, and without the threat of paying interest.

And now, many companies are working to accept cryptocurrencies (aka crypto such as Bitcoin) as a form of payment.

The ways you can transfer your money online to pay for things are changing and will certainly continue to change.

For clarity, don't confuse a credit card with a debit card. Do they both come in plastic rectangular form? Yes. Do they both easily serve as an online payment method? Yes. However, what goes on behind the scenes is drastically different.

Debit cards are linked directly to your checking account. When you use a debit card, money is immediately taken from your bank account balance to pay for your purchase. Debit cards are different from credit cards because when you use a credit card, you are borrowing money from the bank—so you only pay for a credit card purchase when you choose to pay your credit card bill.

Here are some potential perks of having a credit card:

- Rewards programs: Many credit cards offer rewards programs that allow you to earn points, miles, or cash back on purchases that can be redeemed for various benefits.
- Building credit history: Using a credit card responsibly can help you establish and improve your credit score, which is important when applying for loans or other credit products in the future.
- Fraud protection: Credit cards typically offer more robust fraud protection than debit cards, and you are not liable for unauthorized charges.

- Travel benefits: Some credit cards offer travel perks such as free checked bags, airport lounge access, and travel insurance.
- Purchase protection: Many credit cards offer purchase protection in case an item you bought is damaged, lost, or stolen.
- Convenience: Credit cards allow you to make purchases without carrying cash or checks, and they are widely accepted by merchants around the world.

One of the main perks of using a credit card for routine purchases is that issuing banks often offer substantial rewards programs, such as earning points that can be redeemed for cash back or travel. They are able to offer these point systems because they make so much darn money off their customers who are in a lot of debt.

An added benefit touted by many credit cards is the accompanying insurance coverage applied to purchases. For example, a number of credit cards provide various types of travel insurance (including trip cancellation, trip interruption, and car rental loss and damage insurance) when you use your card to pay for flights, rental cars, and other travel expenses. Some will even provide extended warranty protection on certain items you buy. Be wary when you come across a card with a long list of perks though. Chances are it will come with an annual card fee, which may or may not be worth it.

It's not your salary that makes you rich, it's your spending habits.

— Chuck Jaffe, personal finance columnist

The bottom line is that it is okay to have a credit card if you pay off the entire statement balance every month and stick to your planned budget (you have to possess the self-control to handle the power of this tool). If you pay only the minimum balance due each month, you will end up paying very high interest fees to the card company; you must pay the balance off in full prior to the due date, and the best way to go about this is setting up auto pay. Just make sure you have enough in your checking account to cover the monthly statement.

Keeping a Clean Credit Score (And Why You Need One)

In addition to lucrative points systems and easy payment-making, credit cards have one more primary benefit—helping you build your credit score for later, more substantial purchases.

Your credit score is a number ranging from 300 to 850 that lenders use to help them decide how likely it is that they will be repaid on time (or at all) if they let you borrow money through a loan or a credit card. In other words, it tells them how much they can trust you. The higher your credit score is, the less risky you are in the eyes of the lender (that would be the bank or credit card company). So you'll get a lower interest rate, which is what you want.

Lenders will look at your credit score if you one day ask to borrow money to purchase a car, build a house, or take out student loans to get an advanced degree. Your personal credit score is built on your credit history:

- Were your past bills paid on time?
- How much total money do you owe?

- How long have you been borrowing money?
- What kinds of loans do you have?
- When was the last time you asked to borrow money?

When it comes to credit, paying your bills on time is like making a slam dunk in basketball. It's one of the best ways to get your score higher. If you have a credit card, instead of viewing it as a way to borrow money, think of it as a tool to prove to the bank that you are a reliable person to lend to—that way banks will be more likely to charge you less interest when you try to borrow money for the big purchases later in life. Use it for little purchases here and there but always aim to pay your monthly bill in full so that you never owe interest (yes, I realize this is like the tenth time I've repeated this).

It's a good idea to keep tabs on your credit score so that you aren't surprised if and when you apply for a car loan or a house mortgage. Most credit cards offer a service to immediately check your credit score via their online portal—importantly, in a way that does not harm your score (this is called a soft credit check). A soft credit check does not decrease your credit score, but a hard credit check, which is what a formal application for a new credit line will trigger, will slightly decrease your credit score. Frustrating, right?

In my opinion, merely inquiring about loan rates should not be worthy of dinging your credit score, but I don't make the rules. This is the world we live in, so be aware of it. If you're in the United States, you can also get copies of your full credit report by requesting it from each major credit bureau (Experian, Equifax, and TransUnion) every twelve months at AnnualCreditReport.com.

One last thing to cover while on the topic of credit is your credit line, also commonly referred to as the credit limit. A credit card works by allowing you a preset borrowing limit that can be tapped into at any time. For example, if your card's credit limit is $5,000 and you have a balance of $1,500 (in other words, you already spent $1,500), then your remaining available credit is $3,500. Anything you try to purchase above this amount will likely be denied by your credit card company. Some issuers may allow you to spend over your limit to a point, but you may be charged a fee or a higher interest rate.

Good Debt vs. Bad Debt

A big part of making good money management decisions comes down to your mindset on assets and liabilities, and the accompanying concept of good debt and bad debt.

Depending on who you ask, debt can be a contentious topic, even for expert wealth builders. In one camp are those who believe debt should be avoided at all costs, and they encourage cutting up your credit cards and financing nothing. In the other group are those who believe that borrowing other people's money is the best way to leverage your way into financial freedom.

Both mindsets have served people well historically, so it will be up to you to determine where your approach lies. I'll take a middle-of-the-road style here in explaining how different types of debt can be both good and bad.

In general, debt is good when it is used to buy things that go up in value; whereas, debt is bad when it is used to buy things that go down in value. Good debt has the potential to increase your net worth or enhance your life in an important way. Bad debt involves borrowing money to purchase rapidly depreciating assets (a car, for example) or buying items only for the purpose of consumption (an expensive restaurant meal). You may have heard the old adage, "It takes money to make money." It is true that going into good debt can help you generate more income later. Examples of good debt include:

- Education: An investment in college or a technical degree often pays for itself within a few years of entering the workforce, though not all degrees are equal in this regard.
- Business ownership: Borrowing money to start or buy a business can be risky, yet many individuals are successful at venturing out on their own, especially if they pursue something they are knowledgeable about.
- House/real estate: Taking out a mortgage to buy a home in a growing area may end with you selling it for a higher price in the future and allowing you to pocket the profit; rental properties can also be used as a source of income, as long as the money collected from tenants exceeds the costs of the mortgage and other expenses.

Bad debt, on the other hand, is used to purchase things that won't go up in value or generate future income. Examples of bad debt include:

- Cars: Borrowing money to buy a car is not ideal because the vehicle decreases in value substantially the moment it enters your possession.

- Clothes: Using a high-interest credit card to purchase clothing and then allowing the balance to remain long enough to owe interest on it is a horrible investment; most clothes are intrinsically worth less than half of what consumers pay for them.
- Payday loans: These are short-term, often predatory, loans with extremely high interest rates (typically made for amounts less than $500) that are meant to be repaid with the borrower's next paycheck; if you are short on cash, these should be considered your absolute last option.

Having a good grasp of what is acceptable to go into debt for versus what is not can prevent you from making costly mistakes along your financial journey. When I am considering a large purchase, I ask myself (A) Will this enable me to generate more income in the future? and (B) Will the expected annual return exceed the APR of the loan? If the answer to both of these questions is yes, then I will consider going into debt (good debt, in my mind) to finance the purchase.

Tackling Your Moderate Interest Debt

Once your high-interest debts have been addressed with the snowball or avalanche methods, there are a couple of recommended immediate next steps.

At this point, it likely makes sense to direct your extra cash (that huge debt-crushing snowball that was taking up a chunk of your budget) toward shoring up your emergency fund buffer. If you currently only have one month's worth of expenses saved in your emergency fund and no more high-interest debt, consider increasing the fund to three to six months of living expenses. Three months is likely sufficient if you have no dependents (that would be children) who rely on you to provide for them.

The benefit of deepening your emergency fund is that you are effectively distancing yourself even further from your high-interest debt. Sudden expenses that may have caused you to rely on debt in the first place will no longer be an issue as you tap into your beefed-up emergency fund as needed.

Once your emergency fund is expanded, many experts recommend tackling your moderate interest debt next. It is safe to consider anything over a 4 to 5% interest rate in this bucket, but again exclude your mortgage if you have one—that will be saved for later. Often auto and student loans will fit into this category (depending upon the rate your lender gave you).

The methodology of taking care of your moderate interest debts is the same as before: evaluate the merits of the avalanche and snowball methods and their advantages in your own financial and psychological situation and apply accordingly.

If you don't have any debt, congratulations. I hope this chapter served as a helpful reminder to steer clear of bad debt and think carefully about good debt. If you do find yourself deep into debt, don't get bent out of shape over it; think logically, make a plan, and take action NOW while you are young. You don't want to become a negative net worth statistic as you age.

Once you are getting the maximum employer match possible for your 401(k), when your high and medium interest debts are paid off (basically everything but your mortgage, if you have one), and your emergency fund is at full capacity, it is time to start taking advantage of the holy grail of retirement planning—a government-incentivized account type that, if used correctly, can really boost your future financial prospects.

Key Takeaways

- Work toward eliminating your high and medium interest debts through either the avalanche or the snowball methods.
- It is okay to have a credit card (points and insurance perks are a benefit) if you pay off your statement balance in full every month and stick to your planned budget.
- Increase your emergency fund savings to three to six months of living expenses, depending upon your personal situation.

Take Action: Debt Repayment Worksheet

Populate the table with information on all your current debts. If you find yourself with a relatively large number of debts, you may want to make one table for those with high interest (10%+) and one for the rest. In the "Priority to Pay It Off" column, rank the debts in order of which you want to pay off first. You can prioritize based on highest interest rate (Avalanche method) or smallest balance (Snowball method). Remember to exclude your mortgage from this exercise, if you have one.

EXAMPLE (SNOWBALL METHOD)

Name	Interest Rate (APR)	Amount Owed	Typical Minimum Payment	Priority to Pay It Off
Credit Card 1	17.49%	$10,618	$106	4
Credit Card 2	24.99%	$4,366	$40	1
Student Loan	6.80%	$33,500	$350	5
Auto Loan	5.00%	$7,580	$300	3
Personal Loan	8.50%	$6,300	$175	2

Name	Interest Rate (APR)	Amount Owed	Typical Minimum Payment	Priority to Pay It Off
Credit Card 1				
Credit Card 2				
Student Loan				
Auto Loan				
Personal Loan				

Want a free printable copy of this worksheet?
Visit investnowplaylater.com/worksheets

Chapter 5

Begin Saving for Retirement in an IRA

If you've read *A Teenager's Guide to Investing in the Stock Market* by yours truly, you likely have a solid background on what IRAs are used for and understand how powerful a tool they can be in building wealth. You hopefully even have an account open already. If you do have an IRA account but haven't yet contributed to your employer's 401(k) plan or paid down your debts, don't worry yourself by thinking you've done something wrong or out of order.

It's fantastic if you've already started taking advantage of compounded investment returns. If, since originally opening your IRA, you've started working for an employer who offers a 401(k) match or had to take on some temporary debt (student loans or a car loan, for example) while you transitioned into adulthood, consider pausing your contributions to the account until you have checked off the prior steps that we have discussed so far.

If this is your first time hearing the acronym IRA and you have no clue what I'm talking about, prepare for enlightenment!

The Roth IRA

Franklin D. Roosevelt once said, "Taxes are the dues that we pay for the privileges of membership in an organized society." While taxes will be ever present, sometimes the government cuts us some slack—in this case, to encourage people to save. Despite the invention of the 401(k), the US Congress realized that Americans were still having issues saving and investing for retirement, forcing many citizens to have to work late into life because they could not afford to stop getting a paycheck.

To help combat this lack of savings, the US government passed the Taxpayer Relief Act of 1997 and established what is known as a Roth Individual Retirement Account (Roth IRA).

A Roth IRA allows you to add a certain amount of money to an account each year, and then when you eventually retire, you do not have to pay taxes on any of the money you take out (which is huge). This may sound familiar to the Roth 401(k) discussed in chapter 3. They are certainly siblings. Ideally, when you retire, you'll be able to live off the money you have stashed away in your 401(k) and your IRA—yes, you can have both at the same time.

The initial money that you deposit inside of the Roth is called a contribution, and you can transfer contributions directly from your primary bank account as often as you like. One day, when you eventually sell your investments, you will generate earnings (the profits you make in the stock market on top of your initial investment). In a Roth, you can typically pick from a much wider variety of investments than with an employer-sponsored 401(k)—in an IRA, it's your choice.

As mentioned earlier, you are one day going to have to pay taxes on pretty much every aspect of life (if you haven't realized this already). You will pay taxes as a percentage of your job income, taxes on your home, taxes on things you buy, and the list goes on and on. You also must pay taxes on earnings in the stock market. Again, this is called a capital gains tax.

Say you allow your money to grow year after year for a few decades, and then you withdraw from your account to buy a vacation home on the beach. Well, depending on the amount you withdraw, you could be required to pay over 40% of your earnings straight to the government. Poof—gone! That beach house is now half the size you were planning.

Before you get too discouraged, allow me to explain the Roth IRA in more detail. As a Roth IRA account owner, you are exempt from paying capital gains taxes once you are eligible to begin withdrawing money (retirement, beginning at age 59½). The contributions into your account will be added only after you pay income taxes on them (that is, after-tax contributions, again similar to the Roth 401(k)).

In other words, you get the taxes out of the way now, so that you can reap the rewards of your compounded investments later. Once in your account and invested in the market, it can compound for ten, twenty, or thirty-plus years, tax-free. I do not know about you, but I would much prefer to pay my tax percentage on a small number of dollars now, rather than on the millions I will have later.

The Traditional IRA

It is worth noting that there is another type of IRA besides the Roth, and you guessed it—just like how there is a traditional 401(k) and a Roth 401(k), there is a traditional IRA and a Roth IRA. While a Roth IRA allows for after-tax contributions, a traditional IRA allows for pre-tax contributions. This means that whatever money you put into a traditional IRA, you can deduct from your income taxes for that year; however, unlike the Roth, you must pay taxes on all withdrawals once you retire, as it is treated as income.

In summary, a Roth IRA allows you to enjoy more money in the future, while a traditional IRA allows you to enjoy more money today. It is widely accepted that a Roth IRA is the way to go if you will be in a higher tax bracket once you retire and begin to take withdrawals. As a young adult, you fit the bill for this description (you will likely get raises throughout your working career, thus placing you in a higher income tax bracket at retirement).

Here is Table 6, expanded from the earlier version in chapter 3, which marks the major differences in tax treatment between traditional and Roth accounts, expanded to include IRAs in addition to 401(k)s.

Table 6: Taxable Events by Account Type, Expanded for IRAs

	Roth 401(k)	Roth IRA	Traditional 401(k)	Traditional IRA	Taxable Brokerage Account
Earn Money	Taxable Event	Taxable Event			Taxable Event
Investment Goes Up in Value					
Selling for a Profit					Taxable Event
Receive Dividend Payments					Taxable Event
When You Withdraw			Taxable Event	Taxable Event	

At this point, I'm probably sounding like a broken record with all this 401(k) and IRA stuff. Your main takeaways are that as a young adult,

(1) a Roth 401(k) is preferable if your employer offers it, and (2) a Roth IRA is also preferable. At the end of the day, traditionals are fine, too, and would be much better than doing neither, but the Roth is likely optimal for your situation.

Figure 10 illustrates how powerful IRAs can be when it comes to wealth-building. Notice how the Roth IRA slightly edges out the traditional IRA in total wealth creation throughout the course of a forty-year saving period. Here, both people have a salary of $50,000 per year, are taxed the same, and they stash away $6,500 per year. A 9.7% annual return is assumed, along with a 22% tax rate at age twenty-five and a 32% tax rate at age sixty-five. Taxes are applied to the Roth IRA at the time of each recurring contribution and to the traditional IRA at withdrawal.

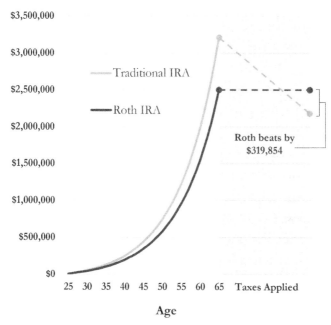

Figure 10: Hypothetical Future Impact of Investing in a Roth Account When Tax Bracket Is Higher at Retirement

Contributing to a traditional IRA will allow for extra money today to invest alongside your retirement accounts, but it will likely be heavily taxed later on. For this reason, the Roth IRA comes out ahead. Also note that for a traditional IRA to have any tax benefits in the year you contribute to it, you typically have to have an earned income less than $73,000 (as of this writing) to claim the full deduction and realize the benefits as illustrated in this example.

Roth IRA Qualifications and Requirements

Okay, so we have determined that a Roth IRA account type is best suited for you—again, primarily because you are starting to invest so early. The specific rules applied to Roth IRAs have changed over time. Check the IRS website (**www.irs.gov**) to get the latest, but here are some account requirements to consider:

- The maximum annual contribution limit for a Roth IRA (as of 2023) is $6,500. You are not allowed to deposit more than the maximum limit into your account for a given tax year. This number is usually adjusted up over time to account for inflation.
- There is a maximum income limit, over which you must phase out of Roth IRA contributions. As of 2023, you cannot earn more than $153,000 per year and still deposit money into a Roth IRA. This requirement is not difficult to meet for most young adults.
- If you withdraw *contributions* before age 59½, you pay no tax or penalty. However, withdrawing *earnings* before age 59½ can mean you owe income tax and about a 10% penalty.

- There is no minimum age to qualify for a Roth IRA.
- The money deposited into a Roth IRA must be earned income.

Depending on your situation, many of these requirements will be of no concern to you. For your age, however, the last point may be the most troublesome, especially if you are attending college and not working full time yet. The amount you contribute to your Roth IRA each year cannot exceed the amount you actually earned from working during the same year. Thus, even if you've saved up a boatload of Grandma's birthday money throughout the years, you can't put it into your new Roth IRA account without working a job.

Fortunately, you can get creative here if you need to, and you might be relieved to know that self-employment counts. According to the Internal Revenue Service, earned income is defined as "wages, salaries, tips, and net earnings from self-employment." Payments for doing lawn care or babysitting count as earned income, and thus qualify for contribution into your Roth IRA account.

But again, you cannot put in more than was earned. If you work part time in your university lab and earned $4,350 throughout the course of the year, you can contribute up to $4,350 to your IRA. Obviously, this requirement is a limiting factor for the partially employed. Put in what you can, but maxing out is ideal.

The question isn't at what age I want to retire, it's at what income.

— George Foreman, professional boxer and indoor grill master

The idea of saving even more for retirement inside of an IRA when you are already putting so much away in your 401(k) may seem like overkill. However, I doubt many people who are entering retirement with million-dollar-plus portfolios think to themselves, "Man, I really wish I would have spent more money on bottomless mimosa brunches and designer handbags."

Even so, while labeled for retirement, money inside of Roth IRAs can actually be tapped whenever you need it, subject to a few rules. There are zero penalties to withdraw the funds you initially put in, but that does not include earnings or interest, which are considered profits. If you start tapping into your earnings, you may be taxed or incur a 10% penalty, depending on your age and situation.

Experts agree it's best not to tap into your Roth IRA funds unless it's absolutely necessary. You want your money to stay in your Roth IRA as long as possible to take advantage of the compounding interest that is accruing.

Deciding What to Invest In

I touched on the stock market earlier when discussing your 401(k), but the topic warrants revisiting in more depth now that we've moved on to the Roth IRA. Why? Because IRA accounts are not restricted to any certain type of funds or stocks. The world is your oyster with an IRA, but this can unfortunately be overwhelming to a new investor. Here is some additional groundwork to build upon what you've learned about investing so far.

Some of the investments you make will be losers—all investors have them. However, if you do your research and narrow down your pool, then invest a portion of your funds by purchasing stock in multiple companies, you will reduce your risk and increase your odds of coming out ahead.

All investments come with risk. Risk refers to the likelihood that you will lose money on an investment. The riskier the investment, the higher the potential reward; the safer the investment, the lower the potential reward. It is a trade-off. For example, if you want the reward of scoring a date to a formal dance, you have to risk a lot of rejection. If you want the reward of becoming an entrepreneur, you have to risk business failure. If you want the reward of becoming a stock market millionaire, you have to risk losing some of your money.

Successful investors find a key balance between risk and reward—usually through the wide net tactic of diversification.

Implementing Diversification

A properly diversified portfolio is made up of investments across all industries of all sizes. This limits your risk while still providing plenty of upside for your money to grow. While you can always pick out and invest in many different companies, one at a time, there are two mechanisms for diversifying your portfolio without having to buy shares of each separate stock yourself: mutual funds and exchange-traded funds (ETFs).

Have you ever gotten a box of chocolates for Valentine's Day? You know what I am talking about, those heart-shaped trays that usually contain a wide variety of flavors for you to try. That is how mutual funds and ETFs can be considered—a package of many different stocks, all wrapped up for you with a bow on top. I will go into further detail on how easy it is to become a stock investor with these two sweet deals; just try not to get a sugar rush.

Mutual Funds

Mutual funds are a collection of stocks that a banker on Wall Street researches and selects for you. When retail (nonprofessional) investors like you and I buy into a mutual fund, our cash is all pooled together. Then, the money manager selects which investments to make. The average mutual fund holds over one hundred different companies, so, naturally, your investment is diversified.

Mutual funds have different goals (which are stated in their prospectus—basically just a summary of their investment strategy). Some seek to focus on capital gains (they buy stocks at low prices and sell them at higher prices), while others focus on companies that pay out high dividends. Some mutual funds focus on certain industries (such as technology, energy, real estate, consumer products, industrials, telecommunication, aerospace, defense). Some mutual funds do not even invest in the stock market but instead track bonds—which are loans to companies or to the government—and other lower-risk securities.

Aside from some minor differences among the choices, you will get a return on your mutual fund investment in the same two ways as if you just owned stock in one company:

1. If the fund sells shares of stock that have increased in price, the profits will be passed on to the investors in the form of a distribution.
2. Dividend payouts are passed on to investors in the form of a distribution.

However, if the fund holdings increase in price but the fund manager decides not to sell them, then the mutual fund's shares themselves increase in price—and thus you can then sell your entire investment to someone else for a profit.

Sounds great, right? You sit back while someone else puts your money to work.

However, as mentioned in my discussion on 401(k)s, you should be extra wary of fees when investing into mutual funds. These fees are referred to as the fund's expense ratio, and as a rule, the more actively managed a fund is (when the manager tries to outperform the broader stock market), the higher the fees they will charge. Fees are charged to your investment as a percentage, and, on average, they will be in the 0.5% to 1.0% range. In the long run, these can start to add up and will eat into the money you make.

Here are some well-known mutual funds:

- Fidelity Investments' Magellan Fund (FMAGX): Perhaps the most renowned actively managed mutual fund because of its long history
- Vanguard Total Stock Market Index Fund (VTSAX): Covers the entire US stock market
- Fidelity Contrafund Fund (FCNTX): Actively managed portfolio of large, undervalued companies with strong earnings growth
- Schwab International Index Fund (SWISX): Tracks non-US companies across Japan, Australia, Germany, France, Switzerland, and the United Kingdom

Exchange-Traded Funds

ETFs are a very similar concept to mutual funds in that they represent a broader group of investments. However, in contrast to most mutual funds' active management, ETFs are passively managed.

ETFs are set up by the folks on Wall Street to track an underlying index (basket of stocks) based on some common criteria, but then they just let them ride. There may be a few tweaks or rebalancing of the fund here and there, but there is very little cherry-picking going on because they are trying to simply match the market, not outperform it. As a result, most ETF fees are lower than mutual fund fees, but they still do exist because there is some cost to operating and managing the fund.

Here are some of the most popular ETFs:

- SPDR S&P 500 (SPY): Tracks the S&P 500 Index, the five hundred largest public companies in the US
- SPDR Dow Jones Industrial Average: Tracks the thirty stocks of the Dow Jones Industrial Average, which aims to represent the American economy
- Invesco QQQ (QQQ): Tracks the Nasdaq 100, which is mostly technology stocks
- iShares Russell 2000 (IWM): Tracks the Russell 2000 small-cap index, representing two thousand of the smallest public companies in the US

You may have noticed the word *index* listed in the names of some mutual funds, as well as ETFs. An index shows the hypothetical performance of a chosen basket of stocks, usually the broader market in some fashion. An index fund is an actual legal entity that is designed to track an index, and these funds can be structured as mutual funds or ETFs. Index funds are generally less actively managed, which in turn will usually result in lower fees.

Figure 11 places mutual funds and ETFs side by side for a clear comparison of the two. Both mutual funds and exchange-traded funds are investment vehicles that pool together money from investors to purchase a portfolio of stocks, bonds, or other assets. However, there are some key differences between the two, including how actively managed they are, the fees they charge, and when their prices change.

There are many mutual fund and ETF screeners available online to help you choose your Roth IRA investing approach. You can search by name, category, or industry and do a side-by-side comparison of historical performance, top holdings (which companies they are most heavily invested in), and expense ratios across similar funds. There are also several rating agencies that rank funds on all of these variables and present them in a way that is easy to compare.

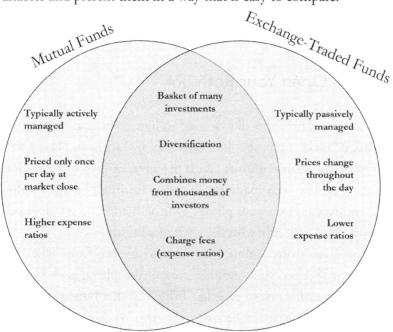

Figure 11: A Comparison of Mutual Funds and ETFs

When you are researching mutual funds and ETFs to decide what to invest in, remember to look for these big three items, which will all be clearly stated on any fund summary page:

1. Historical performance (the average annual return of the fund over the past five, ten, or fifteen-plus years)
2. Expense ratio (what percentage of your money will be lost to fees each year)
3. Diversification (what variety of companies is built into the fund)

Mutual funds and ETFs are both great investment vehicles for beginners (and frankly for investors of all ages) because they track the returns of the stock market and limit risk by building in diversification.

How to Open Your Roth IRA

Not long ago, investors like us used to have to physically walk into a bank or make a phone call to an actual live agent to place a trade and purchase shares of stock. With the advancement of technology, this process has been made much easier. It can all be done online, and even via apps on your phone. During market hours, shares can be purchased instantly with the click of a button.

There are many online platforms to choose from when you open your IRA account, and they are called brokerages. A broker is a matchmaker for investors—they bring together buyers and sellers and facilitate the trade between the two. A brokerage account allows you to buy and sell your investments. Sample platforms as of this writing include E*TRADE, Fidelity, Vanguard, and Charles

Schwab. Make sure the brokerage you are using carries Roth IRAs. Some do not.

When researching brokerages to determine the route you want to take, make sure to compare commissions (fees for buying or selling stock, which are usually charged as a flat rate per order). As of this writing, many brokerages are moving to a commission-free model for stocks and ETFs. Zero-fee trades are becoming the new industry standard. You can find the latest by browsing their different websites—obviously, the cheaper the fees, the better.

Some brokerages that still do charge commissions justify this because they offer more options for technical analysis for more complicated (and more active) trading strategies. For buy-and-hold investing (which is advocated for retirement savings, such as in your new IRA) and for beginners, a commission-free brokerage will likely suffice.

Here is the step-by-step process for opening an account through an online brokerage. Click "Open an Account" on their home page. The whole process should not take more than fifteen minutes. Exact details will differ depending on the brokerage you use, but the general flow of the application will look something like this:

1. **Account Selection:** You will need to choose an account type. The Roth IRA option will most likely be listed with other retirement account options. Make sure you select the correct one.

2. **Personal Information:** Input your general personal details, such as full name, phone numbers, email, and physical address.

3. **Identity Verification:** You will need your Social Security number to open an account. If you are under eighteen, most brokerages will require you to open a custodial account, which means you will need a parent's or guardian's Social Security number in place of yours.

4. **Account Login:** Now that the account is opened, you will be prompted to create a username and password to log in. Build a strong password that is unique to this account and keep it somewhere safe.

5. **Name Beneficiaries:** Most platforms will require you to set beneficiaries, to define who should receive your money if you have an untimely death. Uncomfortable to think about, but necessary. You will likely need to provide their Social Security numbers and birth dates to list them. If listing more than one person, you can usually split out which percentage of your total funds you want to go to each person. Welcome to the world of adulting.

6. **Investing Goals:** Many applications will have you fill out a section on your investing goals, to get a feel for what you are trying to accomplish with your new account. Answer however you think, but do not worry about listing anything incorrectly on this part; it is not terribly pertinent to the setup of your account.

7. **Funding:** Finally, link your checking/savings account and transfer some money in (most will not require a minimum initial deposit, but it depends on the brokerage; this would rarely be more than $500). Once your first contribution is deposited and cleared (this can take a week or so), the time has come to make your first trade.

If you have a steady source of income, consider setting up recurring contributions (once you log in to your account, this will usually be listed in the tab for *Transfers*). Your brokerage will then automatically draft your bank account every month (or every two weeks, or every week) on the dates you select. For example, if you want to contribute a total of $2,400 for the year, then set up a monthly contribution of $200 ($200 x 12 months = $2,400 total).

Also consider turning on your brokerage's dividend reinvestment option. They go by different names depending on the brokerage, but they all perform the same action—they reinvest your dividend payments. Enrolling in a Dividend Reinvestment Plan (DRIP) will automatically take your dividend disbursements and invest them commission-free into additional shares of the same stock (often buying partial shares of the stock). Instead of letting that cash sit idle in your account, why not just reinvest it? More compounding.

Placing an Investment Order

Assuming you already know which investment funds you want to own, you now need to decide how many shares to buy. A relatively easy thing to calculate, simply divide the total amount you wish to put into the company by the most recent stock price. Note that share prices are an ever-moving target, even in the after-hours markets, but usually you will not see any changes too drastic from the time you place the order to the time it gets filled. Do not fret; there is a way to tell your broker the maximum price that you are willing to pay.

If you are putting money into a mutual fund, simply search for the fund you want, click *Buy* and input your desired investment amount, and then click *Place order*. It is really that simple.

There is a little more to it if you are placing an order for an ETF or for individual shares of stock. First, from your account, search for the company/ETF name and pull up its summary page. Click *Buy* to take you to the order form. Here, you will see the *Last Price* listed, which is the price per share. Divide the total amount of money that you wish to invest into the company/ETF by the *Last Price*. This will give you the *Quantity* of shares to input. If your broker does not offer fractional trading (the ability to buy portions of a share), you will need to round up or down to the nearest whole number of shares.

Next, you will need to select a *Price type* (or *Order type*), which will let your broker know what price you are willing to pay for the shares. Do not be intimidated by the different options you see, which will probably look something like this:

Market—buy ASAP at the best available price

Market on close—buy as a market order as close as possible to the close of trading on the day the order is entered

Limit—buy only at a specific price or better (this is how you tell your broker the maximum price that you are willing to pay)

Stop on quote—once your specified price is reached, a market order is executed, and the entire order is filled at the best available price

Stop limit on quote—once your specified price is reached, a limit order is triggered to buy only at a specific price or better

The most commonly used option here is *Market*, and this is all you will likely ever need to select. However, if for some reason you determine that there is a maximum price that you are willing to pay per share, and you do not want the order to be executed unless it is below that price, then it would be best to place a *Limit* order. *Stop* orders are used when you want to wait for the stock to reach a certain price before executing the trade. I rarely use Stop orders.

Once your price type is selected, you will likely need to specify a *Duration* for the order, which will tell your broker how long you want it to remain in effect, until fully executed or canceled. For example, you may be able to select *Good for day*, *Good for 60 days*, or even *Good until date*, and then put in your specific end date. If your price-type criteria are not met by market close on the end date, the entire order will be canceled.

I most commonly place *Good for day* orders. I'm not trying to get fancy here. Once this info is entered, you should be able to complete the purchase, after which you'll notice the cash balance in your account decrease and the ownership of the new shares will be listed in the *Portfolio* section of your account.

The SEP IRA and SIMPLE IRA

Traditional and Roth IRAs are the best known and the most used, but there are a couple of additional types of IRAs that can be used by people in specific situations (similar to how the 401(k) is).

A SEP IRA, which stands for Simplified Employee Pension, allows an employer, like a small business or self-employed individual, to make retirement plan contributions into a traditional or Roth IRA established in the employee's name. This allows the employer to get tax benefits for the effort. The SEP IRA is best for self-employed people or small-business owners with few or no employees. Just be aware that if you're both the employer and employee, it's important to follow SEP IRA rules to avoid running afoul of the IRS.

A SIMPLE IRA is available to small businesses that do not have any other retirement savings plan. Simple stands for Savings Incentive Match Plan for Employees. This plan allows for both employer and employee contributions, similar to a 401(k) plan, but with simpler, less costly administration and lower contribution limits. The SIMPLE IRA is best for smaller companies with fewer than one hundred employees. If you're self-employed, you may be better off opening a SEP IRA for the higher contribution limits.

You can find more information about these plans and how to qualify for them with a quick online search or visit the IRS website.

Automate Your Wealth-Building

In an ideal world, you'll max out your IRA contribution each year, which as of this writing, is $6,500 for a Roth account. While perfectly allowable, you may not have that much cash just sitting around at the beginning of the year to throw into your account all at once (that predictable year-end holiday hangover can really do a number on your budget).

Instead, you can just break it up into periodic contributions and account for this in your monthly budget and cash flow balancing (chapter 1). For example, I like to contribute $541.66 per month to my IRA, and at the end of the year I've completely maxed out.

To make this a set-it-and-forget-it type activity, consider setting up automatic direct deposit each month to shuttle money from your checking account, after your paycheck hits, directly into your new Roth IRA. Many brokerages will allow you to take it a step further and automatically use that cash to purchase your fund of choice. For example, you could set things up so that every month on the fifth, you invest $541.66 in the Vanguard S&P 500 ETF (VOO) by automatically debiting your checking account, depositing it into your Roth IRA, and then converting it into shares of VOO.

If the brokerage you use does not seem to offer this capability, then you will need to log into your account and place an order to actually purchase the fund that you want your money to be invested in. DO NOT ALLOW YOUR MONEY TO JUST SIT IN CASH.

If you don't think a monthly activity like that is best suited for you, no biggie, just contribute it all at the beginning of the year, or the middle of the year, or the end of the year, or split it up into quarterly contributions. The point is, figure out a system that makes you transfer money into the IRA and purchase the shares on a scheduled basis—do this and you are way ahead of most people.

Note, though, that recurring contributions to an investment account on a consistent basis do enable you to take advantage of an added benefit—dollar cost averaging. With this concept, instead of investing all of your available cash for the year as a lump sum on one single day (in any account, not just your Roth IRA), spread it out a little—month by month or week by week. This will help you avoid entering the market at a very high price.

Remember, you want to buy as cheaply as possible. You can average out the day-to-day swings and volatility of the stock market by investing little by little at set intervals. When you look back after having invested the total amount you intended, you will usually find that you have lowered your overall cost basis (average price paid), therefore providing you a better return.

Dollar cost averaging also takes the emotion out of investing, if you stick to the plan. When you start telling yourself, "Well, the news says the market might keep falling, so I'm going to skip a month or two," or something along those lines, do yourself a favor and splash ice-cold water on your face. The news doesn't know what the stock market is going to do tomorrow. Neither do economists, hedge fund managers, or your uncle Jimmy. Invest consistently, expect there to be bumps along the way, and ignore everything else.

Your Roth IRA can be a money-making machine if you get in the habit of contributing as much as possible to it and choosing a diverse group of stocks to invest in, like through an index fund. The key to success will be consistency. Because unlike your employer-sponsored 401(k) plan, an IRA is all you. No deduction straight from your paycheck. You have to possess the discipline to watch the cash hit your checking account and then shuttle it away before you are tempted to spend it. In the end, it will be well worth it (if you agree with me in thinking that bagging millions for your future self is worth it).

If you find yourself at a standstill on your budgeting (as in you don't think you can squeeze anything else out to contribute to a Roth IRA), allow me to remind you that each and every dollar you contribute now will be worth magnitudes more later. For example, if you pick up a side hustle and earn just an extra $280 per month to begin investing in a Roth IRA at age twenty-five, you'll retire at age sixty with $1 million in your account. If you earn $70 per yard you mow, that's only one yard each weekend.

Do what you need to do to MAKE IT HAPPEN. Also consider cutting back on some of your wants and investing the difference. The worksheet at the end of this chapter puts common nonessential expenses into perspective by helping you calculate the opportunity cost of not investing.

A quick note to readers outside of the United States—yes, a lot of this chapter has been devoted to US-specific tax rules and accounts. Similar to the 401(k) situation, I recommend exploring what options your government has available for retirement savings, and contribute money to them in place of this, if applicable. The thought process, tax optimization, fee avoidance, and investment strategy will be the same, but the specific account nomenclature, tax structuring, and rules and requirements will be different.

By the way, congrats on making it this far in the book. Just by making the five steps that I have covered so far the cornerstone of your personal finance strategy, you can be confident that you are well ahead of the average person's financial health, and you have a very high probability of being able to live a dignified retirement where you can tap into your savings once you stop working (or at least stop working for money and start working for fun).

The last two steps will help you in accelerating the path to financial independence so that you reach retirement even sooner, as well as how to approach large spending goals (such as buying a house, higher education, wedding funds, or taking a big vacation) by putting any excess cash you have to work on more advanced strategies.

Key Takeaways

- Try to project whether you expect to be making more money, and therefore sit in a higher tax bracket when you are older and closer to retirement; if you do, then a Roth IRA is likely the preferred account for you to open.
- Saving for the long term in a taxable brokerage account can cost you hundreds of thousands of dollars in taxes that could have been avoided in an IRA.
- If you are expecting any large required purchases or personal investments in the near future (maybe college, professional certifications, advanced degree, a car to get to work), contribute excess savings in an account until the amount needed for these expenses is reached, but try maxing out your IRA account first, if possible.

Take Action: The Future Value of My Vices Worksheet

This exercise is a true eye-opener. Brainstorm some of your vices that cost the most money. If you take the monthly cost and multiply it by the listed factor (which accounts for forty years of compounding), you'll get a pretty good idea of how much money you are costing your future self by not investing it!

EXAMPLE

Vice	Cost per Month	Shortcut Multiplication Factor	Future Value in 40 Years (9.7% interest
Going Out on Weekends	$275	x 4896	$1,346,400
Golf Club Membership	$200	x 4896	$979,200
Late-Night Food Delivery	$80	x 4896	$391,680
Weekday Coffee Orders	$60	x 4896	$293,760

Vice	Cost per Month	Shortcut Multiplication Factor	Future Value in 40 Years (9.7% interest
Going Out on Weekends		x 4896	
Golf Club Membership		x 4896	
Late-Night Food Delivery		x 4896	
Weekday Coffee Orders		x 4896	

Want a free printable copy of this worksheet?
Visit investnowplaylater.com/worksheets

Chapter 6

Plan Your Financial Independence

ecause you are just now entering the workforce, it may be difficult for you to fathom wanting to retire. If you are starting
a new job, you probably have a lot of enthusiasm for your work,
especially if it is in a field that you've studied for and are passionate
about. Well, not to rain on your parade, but chances are that feeling
won't last.

According to a 2022 Gallup study, 60% of Americans reported
being emotionally detached at work and 19% as being miserable.
I don't mean to be cynical here, I just want to prepare you for the
reality of what may be coming.

I'm going somewhere with this thought process—somewhere
called financial freedom. If, and when, you are inevitably passed up
for that well-deserved promotion, forced to report to an inhuman
robot for a boss, or just sick and tired of the seemingly purpose-
less responsibilities day after day, you'll be grateful if you have the
financial wherewithal to part ways with your employer and venture
out on a new path. Financial freedom will enable you to walk out
the door.

In this chapter, I will first cover the topics of saving for near-term spending goals and accelerating retirement savings inside your 401(k). Then, I will discuss what can be done to retire early.

Set Aside for Near-Term Spending Goals

After your IRA is maxed out, but before continuing to work toward financial independence, do some thinking on whether you are expecting any large required purchases or personal investments in the near future (such as buying a house or starting a business). If so, put aside your excess savings in a savings account until the amount needed for these expenses is reached.

A lot of what I've been preaching so far in this book is save, save, save, but please also don't forget to *live your life*. If you've accomplished the prior steps and have some things you'd like to spend money on, treat yourself. You deserve to let off the gas a little, just don't overdo it. You don't want to unwind your progress thus far. Your first step at getting back at it will be with a push to increase how much you set aside for retirement across all of your accounts.

Increase Retirement Savings to 15% of Salary

At this point in your financial journey, it's a good idea to revisit your 401(k) and evaluate whether you should be contributing more money to it each month. Most professionals recommend a target of 15% of your income being set aside specifically for retirement each year. To calculate how your current savings rate compares, add up your 401(k) contribution plus your Roth IRA contribution.

Divide the result by your income and multiply by 100 to convert it to a percentage.

Note that what your company matches, what your pension is, or what your military retirement is does not enter into that equation. Target contributing the 15% yourself for the most conservative approach to retirement planning, and anything else thrown in by your employer, or others, can be considered the cherry on top.

For example, if you earn $80,000 per year and currently contribute $4,800 per year to your Roth 401(k), receiving your maximum employer match of 3% ($2,400), plus you max out your Roth IRA at $6,500 per year, you can calculate your total retirement savings rate as follows:

$$\frac{401(k)+IRA}{Annual\ Salary} = \frac{\$4,800+\$6,500}{\$80,000} = \frac{11,300}{\$80,000} = 0.14$$

$$\textbf{0.14} \times \textbf{100 = 14\% Current Contribution}$$

In this example, you are currently saving 14% of your income for retirement, versus a goal of 15%. How do you figure out how much additional to throw into your 401(k) each month to hit this target? Try this equation next:

$$\frac{\left(\dfrac{15\%\ Target - X\%\ Current}{100}\right) \times Annual\ Salary}{12\ Months} =$$

$$\frac{\left(\dfrac{15\% - 14\%}{100}\right) \times \$80,000}{12\ Months} = \begin{array}{l}\textbf{\$66.67/\textit{mo}} \\ \textbf{\textit{Add'l. Contrib.}}\end{array}$$

To hit your retirement savings target of 15% in this example, you'll need to tell your employer to take an additional $66.67 per month from your paychecks and deposit it into your 401(k) for you. Keep in mind, if you have already unlocked the maximum match your employer offers, they won't be contributing anything extra in association with what you add here, but that's okay. It's great that you took advantage of the match earlier, but now it's time to go above and beyond to secure your retirement. Note, if you are a high earner and you max out your 401k ($22,500 as of this writing) and IRA ($6,500) each year and still haven't met the target, set up a dedicated taxable brokerage account and contribute to it until you reach the 15% retirement savings goal.

The same applies to the alternative retirement accounts. If your employer does not offer a 401(k), increase your contributions to a similar plan such as a 403(b), individual 401(k), SEP IRA, or SIMPLE IRA to reach 15% pretax income saved. If you are ineligible for even these, contribute to a taxable brokerage account to reach the 15% retirement savings target. Note that you may need to save more if you are behind on retirement savings.

Check out the graph in Figure 12, which shows the potential future value of someone who makes $50,000 per year and saves 15% of their salary for retirement (split between a 401(k) and IRA), starting at age twenty-five. A 3% annual pay raise is assumed for the purposes of this projection, as well as a 9.7% compounding rate to match the historical performance of the S&P 500 index.

Also, there is NO employer match assumption built into this model—if this person had a match and took advantage of it, they'd have even more money at retirement. In total, they contributed a little under $600,000 to the accounts, but because it was invested, that money multiplied itself into over $5 million. That sure is a lot of zeros! Oh, and don't forget, if this money was contributed to Roth accounts (401(k) + IRA), it's all tax-free when they go to withdraw it.

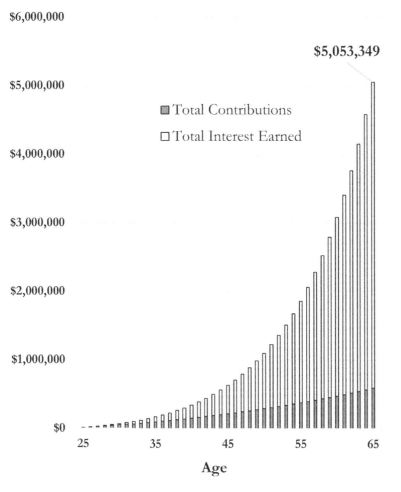

Figure 12: The Future Value of Saving and Investing 15% of Gross Salary for Retirement

The investments inside your Roth 401(k) and Roth IRA will provide ample benefits for you later on in life, but if you desire to retire earlier than age 59½ (the age when you can begin withdrawing earnings without being subject to a 10% early-withdrawal fee), you will need to begin allocating excess money to more flexible investment accounts, even if they won't have the wonderful tax benefits of 401(k)s and IRAs.

Don't Rely on Social Security

If you are working in America, you've likely noticed that the government takes a portion of each of your paychecks in the form of FICA taxes (Federal Insurance Contributions Act) to fund Social Security and Medicare programs. In total, the tax is around 15% with half being paid by you and the other half paid by your employer. In essence, the US has designed this system so that you pay into the program throughout your working career via these taxes, and then when you enter retirement in your sixties you can begin collecting checks from the government via Social Security and health insurance benefits via Medicare.

Is it possible to sustain yourself with just Social Security at retirement? Don't count on it.

Social Security benefits are intended to replace only 40% of your preretirement income. Experts suggest that you will need 70% to 80% of your preretirement income to live comfortably during retirement, which creates a gap of 30%, or more, to fill.

To address this gap, you must establish reliable retirement income streams through various means, including 401(k) or IRA savings. It is also tough to assume with any certainty that Social Security will still exist in its current form by the time you retire. Your best bet is to take matters into your own hands. Start saving early, invest often, and think of your Social Security benefits as an added bonus.

Plan for Early Retirement (If Desired)

Being financially independent means that you could continue living your current lifestyle without ever having to work again. The motivation to achieve this status is different from person to person and may not be as dramatic as my earlier bad boss example.

Some people truly desire to retire early and get the break from work, along with enjoying the accompanying leisure activities; some have a passion project that they are desperately ready to let blossom without the added pressure of needing a job to bring in enough money to make ends meet; yet others still are perfectly content in their current jobs, they just want the reassurance of financial stability to fall back on just in case a worst-case scenario unfolds like job loss or illness.

Quantitatively, most experts will identify you as being financially independent when you have accumulated at least 25 times your annual living expenses in the form of savings and investments. For example, if you require $50,000 per year to live comfortably, then your financial independence (FI) number is $50,000 x 25 = $1,250,000.

Why is the magic FI factor 25? Aside from being an easy number to remember, there is some proven math behind it too. The way you can live off a certain amount of money forever without adding to it is if it grows itself each year by being invested (also called passive income). Specifically, if you hit your FI number as calculated here, the general rule of thumb is that you will be able to withdraw 4% of the money per year for spending, indefinitely.

There are certain strategies to concern yourself with on how to handle the lump of money once you hit your FI number, but that's for another book. Focus on getting there first, which is the hard part.

The Lowdown on Taxable Accounts

Taxable accounts, while quite simple, can sometimes be a point of confusion for people navigating the intricacies of financial decision-making. When you hear someone call their investment account a standard account, a regular brokerage account, or a taxable account, they are all referring to the exact same thing.

A taxable brokerage account can do everything your other accounts can do, plus more. In these accounts, brokerages allow you to purchase individual stocks, ETFs, mutual funds, bonds, certificates of deposit (you may know them as CDs, and these are not music discs), and others. Whatever your heart desires.

Most brokerages will also allow you to play around with futures, options contracts, and margin trading—beware of these, they are the tools of a full-time day trader, not an up-and-coming young professional with an eye toward long-term wealth creation via buy-and-hold investing. Stick to things you understand.

If you open and invest inside of a taxable brokerage account, you will of course have to pay attention to your taxes, because everything you do inside of the account will be subject to the standard tax law—unfortunately there will be no incentives here like the IRA and 401(k).

As mentioned earlier, when you sell a stock, ETF, or mutual fund for a profit, you will have to pay a capital gains tax on the proceeds. The specific amount depends on how long you held onto it (in the US, at least). You'll also have to pay taxes on the dividends you receive inside a taxable brokerage. All these details may be making it hard to understand why you would ever open an account like this.

Taxable brokerage accounts are worth looking into for two reasons.

1. Accounts such as 401(k)s and IRAs have maximum contribution limits; if you want to invest more money than that, you'll need to turn to a taxable account.
2. There is ample flexibility with investing in a taxable account because there is no penalty for early withdrawal; this enhances the liquidity of what is invested inside the account.

Speaking of liquidity, this is a concept that is worth diving into.

Maintaining Liquidity

Contrary to popular belief, increasing your financial liquidity does not entail dunking your wads of cash into a bucket of water and then stuffing the soaking wet bills into your wallet. Rather, liquidity is a measure of how quickly you are able to convert your assets into cash. The higher your personal liquidity, the easier it is to meet your financial obligations.

If you want to turn your Babe Ruth autographed baseball into cash, what would be the process? You'll need to (1) conduct research on the ball to evaluate its condition, who owned it, and what era it's from, (2) send the ball to a certified sports authentication company, (3) receive your ball back with an accompanying certificate of authenticity, (4) have the ball appraised by a memorabilia dealer, and (5) sell the ball by attending a trade show or auctioning it off online. Sports memorabilia and collectors' items are not at all liquid—turning them into cash typically takes a lot of time and effort.

Selling a share of stock or an ETF, on the other hand, is quite quick and simple, and thus they are very liquid investments. When you sell a share of stock, the official transfer of the cash value to your account is called the settlement. For most stock trades, settlement happens two business days after the trade is executed. Not too bad. But what is even more liquid than stocks? Try your savings and checking accounts—you can use the cash virtually instantly.

Liquidity has nothing to do with how much an asset is worth, but rather how easily you can access its full value. More specifically, the quicker you can access the value, for as cheaply as possible (and with low fees), and for as fair a market value as possible.

A key consideration in evaluating liquidity is whether the asset can be converted to cash and still maintain its value. For example, if you try to sell your car to someone, they could easily begin to haggle with you over the hairline scratches on its door handle. The face value of the car may be $20,000, but you have to sell it for $18,000 just to close the deal, thus bucketing the asset in the illiquid category.

Generally, *liquid* investment assets include

- Cash
- Money market funds
- Bonds
- Stocks
- ETFs

While *illiquid* investment assets include

- Art
- Wine/whiskey

- Antiques
- Real estate
- Coin collections
- Classic/vintage cars

Liquidity is an important concept for up-and-coming investors to learn because at some point you will want to be able to access the wealth that you build. If all of your assets are tied up in long-term investments with early-withdrawal penalties (for example, retirement accounts), you may find yourself cash poor at a time of need.

One particular account may come to mind when you think of having liquidity and needing cash quickly—your emergency fund. Additionally, you'll have ample liquidity in your taxable brokerage account (circling back to why liquidity was brought up in the first place).

Conclusion: To quit your day job way before you reach your sixties, you'll need to achieve financial independence, which will require you to have a fairly liquid investment portfolio, which will require you to open a taxable brokerage account that you can tap into as needed without any rules and penalties.

There is, however, another important component in the path to financial freedom, aside from just amassing a sum of liquid investments in a brokerage account—creating sources of passive income.

Converting Earned Income into Passive Income

A pivotal moment in your investing career will occur when you realize how to generate passive income. Putting in hard work now to be able to just sit back and watch the checks roll in later is a very satisfying journey.

Do you recall my discussion on cash flow from the budget creation process? If you're retiring early, you'll need to have enough cash flow to cover your living expenses each month, and while, yes, you'll be able to tap roughly 4% of your taxable brokerage account each year to take care of this if you have one, you'll also find it handy if you have income coming in from other sources.

Passive income is money generated from investments, properties, or side hustles. These all definitely require time and (typically) money to get started, but once you put in the work, the big payoff will be down the road, especially if you can scale, automate, and outsource the day-to-day operations required to maintain production of the income, thus qualifying it as truly passive. You may want to:

- **Create a dividend portfolio.** Have companies cut you a check every quarter; you can search out and hand select your own choices of the highest paying (and most reliable) stocks, or you can purchase a dividend-focused ETF.
- **Own a rental property.** If running numbers, finding tenants, and keeping maintenance under control are something you think you'd be good at, try your hand at real estate investing.
- **Buy into a private equity fund.** Investing in a private business that you expect to generate future income is often a risky, long-term bet; these types of deals are usually only available to high-net-worth individuals so you may need to wait a few years before going for it.
- **Create content and monetize it.** This one covers a lot of opportunities to mix what you're passionate about with

what people value—for example, creating an online course, writing a book, building a blog, selling photography, and running sponsored posts on social media (calling all influencers).

- **Rent out a part of your home short term.** Airbnb makes this passive income stream pretty efficient to get started on, especially if you already have a spare bedroom.
- **Start or buy a local business.** Starting a new business is admirable, but statistically, most don't last past a couple of years; buying an already established business, however, offers you the potential to generate cash flow right from the beginning; then put a good manager in place to run it for you to make it passive.

No matter what direction you go, just remember that your investment needs to have a positive contribution to your monthly cash flow, meaning it turns a profit for you.

> *The key to financial freedom and great wealth is a person's ability to convert earned income into passive and/or portfolio income.*

— Robert Kiyosaki, author of *Rich Dad Poor Dad*

Achieving Financial Independence

Now, I want to provide you with a realistic example of how a person could achieve financial independence and retire early—really early. Will it be without sacrifice? No. If this stuff were super easy, everyone would do it. It takes extreme discipline, goal setting, and, frankly, a burning desire to be able to achieve financial independence by a young age like fifty-five, forty-five, or even thirty-five.

Here's an example of someone named Jonah who is twenty-three years old and saves and invests 50% of his income each year. Jonah makes $50,000 per year at his full-time job. After hours and on the weekends, he owns and operates a landscaping company that he started while he was in college; the small business brings in $20,000 per year in profit. With a total after-tax annual income of $70,000, this means he is living off $35,000 per year—not a life of luxury, but certainly not impossible with thrifty spending habits, especially if located in a low-cost-of-living area.

If we model what Jonah's financial future looks like, assuming he follows all the steps thus far in this book, things can be reasonably expected to shake out like this:

- **Year 1:** Jonah saves $35,000 (one-month emergency fund of $2,917 + $3,000 in Roth 401(k) to get employer's 3% match + $8,000 to pay off credit card debt + $21,083 toward paying off a student loan).
- **Year 2:** Jonah saves $35,000 ($13,917 to pay off remainder of student loan + $6,500 to max out Roth IRA + $4,000 Roth 401(k) contribution to meet 15% total retirement account savings goal + $5,834 to beef up emergency fund to three-months of expenses + $4,166 to a savings account earmarked for a near-term new car purchase).
- **Year 3:** Jonah saves $35,000 ($10,500 toward 401(k) & IRA retirement accounts + $19,417 to purchase the new

(gently used) car + $5,083 to open a financial independence, taxable brokerage account).

- **Year 4:** Jonah saves $35,000 ($10,500 toward retirement accounts + $24,500 to FI brokerage account).
- **Years 5 through 20:** Jonah repeats, with $24,500 yearly contributions dedicated toward reaching financial independence in a brokerage account and $10,500 dedicated to his 401(k) and IRA for tax-free growth.

Jonah lives on $35,000 per year, so to calculate his FI number, we simply multiply by 25, resulting in $875,000. At the beginning of year 20, at just forty-two years old, Jonah has $966,178 in his FI-dedicated brokerage account, which puts him above the FI threshold and provides him enough money to retire early—twenty-three whole years earlier than the average American, in fact.

Then, assuming Jonah keeps that money invested, he should be able to live it up and withdraw up to $85,800 per year for spending, all the way until he passes at age one hundred, as shown in Figure 13. Now I call that a good life.

Of course, there were some simplifying assumptions built into this example—namely, we assumed Jonah never increased his income over the twenty-five years modeled (which is very rare). We also assumed that Jonah's living expenses remained the same (also unlikely, considering inflation and especially if Jonah decided to start a family). These two variables could reasonably cancel each other out, however. Also note that the $85,800 withdrawals that Jonah takes are taxable when he sells off the investments within his account, so his effective take-home income will be a bit lower, yet arguably still very livable.

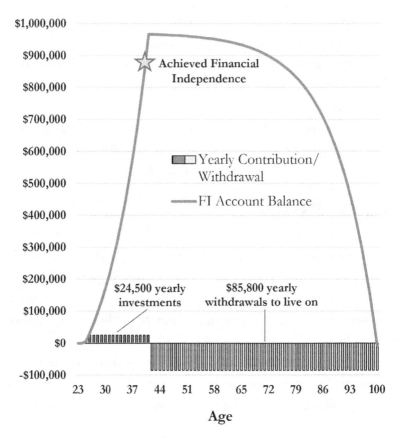

*Figure 13: Jonah's Achievement of Financial Independence and
Ability to Live Off the Account until Age One Hundred*

At age forty-two, Jonah will theoretically be able to tell his boss adios and kick the lawn mower to the curb once he reaches his financial independence number, and his portfolio will automatically replenish itself and, for some time, likely keep growing, because it is invested in the stock market.

Aside from starting earlier, what are the ways that Jonah could have sped up his early retirement? Either (a) reducing his expenses, or (b) increasing his income. Expenses can only be reduced so much, but income is limitless. If he were able to scale his lawn care business, for example, by hiring other workers and marketing his services to get new business, he may have been able to earn more, and subsequently save and invest more, leading to an even earlier retirement.

You may be questioning what will happen to all that money that Jonah was contributing to his Roth 401(k) and Roth IRA throughout the years. Assuming he stopped putting money into them at age forty-two and never touched them again until age sixty, the accounts would then be worth a whopping $3.4 million total, tax-free.

This money is just the proverbial icing on the cake because he's already living off the funds in his brokerage account. Maybe he'll buy a ranch, send all his kids to Ivy League universities, or start his dream business. Who knows? The main thing is that he now has the FREEDOM to do whatever he wants.

Good Habits, Bright Future

Remember, once you reach at least 15% of your income going toward your tax-incentivized 401(k) and Roth IRA accounts each month, things are looking really, really bright for the future. You know you'll have millions in the bank when you retire around age sixty to sixty-five.

But if you still have some spare cash flow now, and early retirement is on your to-do list, set up that taxable brokerage account and add as much money to it as possible. Buy index ETFs to invest in your fair share of the stock market at very low fees, and watch it begin to grow toward your target FI number. You'll be able to access that money much earlier than within a tax-incentivized account.

Also consider how you can convert some of your earned income into passive income. At a certain point in your finance journey, it will begin to be much easier to grow income than to reduce expenses. You'll just need to unlock your creativity. If you buy assets, they will pay you money to own them. If you buy liabilities, they will cost you money to own them. That's a key difference that bears repeating. The Path to Retirement worksheet at the end of this chapter will assist you in laying out your dedicated retirement contributions and calculating whether you need to course correct to get back on track.

In the next chapter, I'll take a look at tax-advantaged college savings plans and HSAs, as they may be useful tools for your situation. A general approach to saving for more immediate spending goals will also be discussed. If you fall into the group that doesn't have extra cash after hitting the 15% retirement goal, you may be feeling left out—you have spending goals, too, like buying a new car, owning a home, and saving for a wedding. It can be difficult to prioritize where your money should be directed, especially once you get to this mature stage of finance management. Let's discuss some of the more advanced methods next.

Key Takeaways

- Aim to save and invest 15% of your pre-tax salary across all your retirement account types and you'll be well on your way to a very secure retirement.
- Find your FI number by multiplying your yearly expenses by 25; this is how much you need in the bank to be able to live off it indefinitely.
- If you want to retire early, consider opening a taxable brokerage account to save and invest your spare cash until you reach your FI goal.

Take Action: Path to Retirement Worksheet

Use this worksheet to answer the question of "Am I saving enough for retirement." These are rules of thumb, but they are a great starting place for determining whether you are on the right track.

Calculate your retirement savings rate

Pretax Income (aka Gross Income): $_____

Annual 401k Contribution: $_____

Annual IRA Contribution: $_____

Annual Brokerage Account Contribution (for retirement): $_____

Sum of Annual Retirement Savings: $_____

Retirement Savings Rate:
(Sum of Annual Retirement Savings / Pretax Income) x 100 = ___%

If your Retirement Savings Rate is less than 15%, increase contributions in this order:

1. Achieve maximum 401k match, if your employer offers one.
2. Max out your IRA contribution.
3. Max out your 401k contribution.
4. If still under 15% income (which means you're making over ~$200k/yr), contribute to a taxable brokerage account until you reach the 15% savings rate.

Calculate your financial independence number

Total Monthly Expenses: $_____

Financial Independence Number:
(Total Monthly Expenses x 12 x 25) = $_____

This is the amount of readily-accessible savings you need to have in order to reach financial independence (and "retire" early).

Want a free printable copy of this worksheet?
Visit investnowplaylater.com/worksheets

Chapter 7

Save for Other Goals and Deploy Advanced Methods

Up until someone reaches a certain age, it is difficult to argue that the average American should be approaching their money management differently than the previously outlined steps (considering the current state of government tax regulations and historical economic growth), but as a person ages, life tends to get more complicated, and the most optimal path becomes less clear.

Having kids, needing to take care of relatives, wanting to buy a house, and the desire to go back to school all cost a good deal of money and may be on your mind. At this point it is safe to say that personal finance really gets personal. You have some options on how to proceed, and it is completely up to you and your own goals and desires.

But consider this: you still need to be educated on those options and the financial consequences of each and have a plan for how you will keep on track for retirement and, of course, continue to live within your means. If you have completed all of the preceding steps and still have income left over, you are in great shape. Here are options to explore when you have some extra, unearmarked cash in your monthly budget.

Treat this chapter like an à la carte menu. There are several important stand-alone topics that have not thus far gotten the attention they deserve. Familiarize yourself with these following concepts. Even if they are not useful to you now, you will likely come across them at some point soon.

Health Savings and Flexible Spending Accounts

In addition to a 401(k), many US-based employers will allow you to enroll in a Health Savings Account (HSA) or Flexible Spending Account (FSA). HSAs and FSAs are accounts you can save money within and then use to pay for healthcare-related costs such as copays, medical bills, and vision expenses.

The money that you contribute to an HSA account is pretax (you won't have to pay income tax on the amount you save), similar to a traditional 401(k). It also grows tax-free, similar to a Roth 401(k). With an HSA, you get the best of both worlds. In fact, many experts tout the triple tax savings of an HSA in that

- funds are tax-free going into the account;
- money grows tax-free; and
- investment earnings and withdrawals for qualified medical expenses are also tax-free.

Another key benefit of HSAs is that the money you contribute to it rolls over from one year to the next. This means that even if you are currently fairly healthy and don't spend much on medicine or doctors' visits, you can begin saving now for when you get older or if you start a family, at which point medical expenses tend to increase.

So what's the catch?

First, there's an annual contribution limit. Second, you must have a high-deductible health plan (HDHP) to qualify. Some large employers have negotiated health plans for their employees that are "too good," if you will, and have no high-deductible plans available. For example, for 2023, the IRS defines a high-deductible health plan as any plan with a deductible of at least $1,500 for an individual or $3,000 for a family. You can check the latest rules at www.healthcare.gov or www.irs.gov.

If you don't qualify for an HSA because you have a low-deductible health plan (whether by choice, that is, you currently make many trips to the doctor, or by requirement, because your employer does not offer anything with a high deductible), an FSA may be your next best option.

An advantage of an FSA is that the funds are available to you beginning on day one. For example, if you expect to spend $2,400 on upcoming medical expenses and thus enroll in an FSA plan with monthly contributions of $200, you'll still have access to use the full annual amount as soon as you're enrolled. And like an HSA, because the account is funded with pretax money, you'll save about thirty cents on each dollar of all eligible healthcare bills.

The big drawback with FSAs, however, is that you typically must "use it or lose it." This means that you need to use all the funds in your FSA by the end of the plan year or forfeit what's left. This clearly puts your budgeting skills to the test.

Generally, you cannot have an HSA and FSA at the same time, barring a couple of exceptions such as dependent care FSAs and limited purpose FSAs.

In summary, once you meet your 15% retirement savings goal, check whether your health insurance plan is high deductible. If so, you may be eligible for an investable HSA, and it may be wise to max out your yearly contributions.

Interestingly, some employers even treat HSAs like they do 401(k)s, offering to match employee contributions up to some predetermined amount. If you don't qualify for an HSA, consider contributing to an FSA to reduce your taxable income for the year. Table 7 lays out the typical requirements, maximums, and other logistics for HSAs and FSAs. It's important to do your research to figure out which account is best for you. To learn more, contact your employer's benefits manager.

Table 7: Health Savings Accounts versus Flexible Spending Accounts

	HSA	FSA
What is it?	Bank accounts that allow for tax-free payment or reimbursement of eligible medical expenses	Employer-established benefit plans that allow for tax-free reimbursement of qualified medical expenses
Who is eligible?	Must be enrolled in an HSA-qualified high-deductible health plan (HDHP) with no other major medical coverage	All employees, not self-employed
Who owns the account?	Employee	Employer
How much can be contributed?	As of 2023, the IRS annual limit is $3,850 for individual and $7,750 for family coverage	Determined by employer, but as of 2023, cannot exceed the annual limit of $3,050
Do the funds carry over to next year?	Yes	Determined by the employer
Is account portable after termination of employment?	Yes. Continued access to unused account balance if the employee is no longer working for the employer	No. Account cannot be maintained if the employee is no longer working for the employer

College Savings Plans (529s)

If you have children (or plan to) and wish to help pay for some or all of their college expenses, consider saving and investing within a 529 plan. A 529 plan is a tax-advantaged investment account in the United States to encourage saving for future education-related costs such as college, K–12 tuition, apprenticeship programs, and even student loan repayments. And fortunately, if using a 529 plan to save for college, the savings will have a minimal impact on financial aid eligibility.

Your 529 savings plan will work much like a Roth IRA or Roth 401(k) in that you can invest your contributions in mutual funds or ETFs and the money will grow tax-free. Contributions are not deductible from your federal income taxes. The real tax benefit is in the future when you begin to withdraw to pay for school expenses. *However*, depending on where you live, some states offer state income tax deductions and/or state tax credits for 529 plan contributions—an added perk.

Once you decide to open a 529, you'll soon realize that nearly every state has at least one plan available. For example, Alabama's plan is called "CollegeCounts," Kentucky's is called the "KY Saves 529," and California's is called the "ScholarShare 529."

Interestingly, you are not limited to using your home state's plan, so it is recommended to search for the lowest-fee plan that you are eligible for before opening an account. It is often recommended to go ahead and get the plan for your state if you can take a deduction, but if you can't, the state sponsorship doesn't much matter aside from investment options and fees.

Fortunately, there are no annual 529 plan contribution limits, but if you ever want to make a very large contribution (around

$15k-plus in one year), you may experience some impacts to your lifetime estate and gift tax exemption, so perform your research first. Also note that each state has an aggregate contribution limit of up to about $500,000 depending on the price of education programs and room and board in the area.

When you go to set up your 529 account, with whichever state's program you choose, you will be asked to designate a beneficiary. If you aim to begin saving funds for a future child who isn't even born yet, you can do so by naming yourself as the beneficiary now and changing it to your future family member (or any other qualifying family member) later.

If you want to fully cover the cost of a future child's college education at a private university, assuming four years of study, a 9.7% annual investment return, and average yearly college cost increase of 2.1%, you only need to contribute $325 per month to a 529 plan, beginning at the birth of the child. That's less than $11 per day to fully fund attendance at the average private university. For the average in-state public school, your estimated monthly contribution drops to only $165, or less than $6 per day.

As with all investing accounts, you'll need to ensure that you select the intended investment option when you add money to your 529 plan. You don't want it to just sit there as cash. For your best shot at achieving that historical average of 9.7% annual compounded returns, find a plan that offers funds tracking the S&P 500 or a similar total market index.

Immediate Spending Goals

If you are like most of us, you probably have some near-term spending goals in mind. Things like buying a house, saving for a new vehicle, fully paying off the mortgage on an existing home, or going on a vacation often fit into this category. Depending on how soon in the future you want to spend money on these items, you may want to try putting your money to work by investing it while it accumulates from your occasional deposits.

Many experts will tell you that for your more immediate spending goals, such as those needed within the next three to five years, you should keep the money set aside in a cash or money market account, which is readily accessible. Aim for the highest interest rate you can get.

For spending goals more than three to five years away, you may want to invest the funds you've saved thus far in a conservative mix of stocks and bonds. Why? Well, recall that investments that reward you with the higher potential for growth always come with a greater degree of risk, especially in the short term. In the stock market, for example, your chance of losing money if invested for a five-year period is only 12%, but the chance of you losing increases to 27% if invested for only one year. The last thing you want is to save a significant amount of money for a big goal only to watch it lose half of its value right when you are about to use it.

And now, to discuss my personal favorite spending goal—saving for a dream vacation. Here's a pic of yours truly on a once-in-a-lifetime solo backpacking trek in Patagonia (Figure 14). See, you *can* save money for your future and have fun in the present. It's all about budgeting and balance.

Now, would I have taken that trip if I had any high-interest credit card debt? Hell no. Pay off your debt, then reward yourself with a trip. It is too dangerous to do the other way around.

Figure 14: Dedicate Your Immediate Spending Goals to What's Most Important to You

And this brings up a great point—you've got to take a look at your budget before pursuing an immediate spending goal. It's super important to assess your income and expenses to get a clear picture of how much money you have available to put toward the goal.

Then, there are other financial aspects of the purchase to consider. For example, when buying a new vehicle, you must consider the operating costs beyond the purchase price. Costs like fuel, insurance, maintenance, and repairs will add up, and some vehicles have higher operating costs than others, so it is important to research these costs before making a purchase. In particular, luxury vehicles and sports cars tend to have higher insurance rates than economy cars. The worksheet at the end of this chapter will walk you through the thought process of buying a car so that you don't end up with something you cannot afford.

Knowing When You Can Afford a House

A particularly common question from young adults is whether buying a house is a good decision, as well as whether it is feasible. Buying a house is a big financial decision that requires careful consideration and planning. Before you start looking at properties, it's essential to determine if you're financially ready to take on the responsibility of homeownership. Let's explore the factors that determine your ability to afford a house and how to assess your readiness to buy.

First, as when evaluating your budget's bandwidth for goals such as buying a car or going on vacation, it's important to determine if you have enough money left over each month to make a mortgage payment. Assuming you are currently renting, you can compare the costs of each since the mortgage will replace rent in your hypothetical future homeowner budget.

Next, calculate your debt-to-income ratio. This ratio is an important factor in determining if you can afford to buy a house as it's used by lenders to assess your ability to repay a loan by comparing your monthly debt payments to your income.

To calculate your debt-to-income ratio, add up all your monthly debt payments, including your car loan, credit card payments, and student loan payments. Then, divide that number by your gross income, which is the amount you earn before taxes and other deductions.

A debt-to-income ratio of around 36% or less is considered to be healthy. This means that no more than 36% of your gross income is going toward debt payments. If your debt-to-income ratio is higher than 36%, it may be difficult to qualify for a mortgage or to secure a low interest rate.

Your credit score is another important factor to consider when determining if you can afford to buy a house. Recall that your credit score is a numerical representation of your creditworthiness, and it's used by lenders to assess your ability to repay a loan. A good credit score is usually considered to be 700 or above. If your credit score is lower than 700, it may be difficult to qualify for a mortgage or to secure a low interest rate.

To improve your credit score, you can pay down any outstanding debt, pay your bills on time, and avoid applying for new credit.

Once you believe you'll qualify for a mortgage, it's time to save for a down payment. A down payment is the initial payment you make toward the purchase of a house and it is usually required by the lender. The typical down payment for a conventional loan is 20% of the purchase price, but some lenders may accept as little as 3% for a government-backed loan.

Saving for a down payment can take time, but there are several ways to make it happen. One option is to set up a dedicated savings account and make regular contributions. Another option is to look into down payment assistance programs, which can help you save for a down payment.

After your down payment is secured, you'll also need to do your research and decide between a fifteen-year loan (with a higher monthly payment) and a thirty-year loan (with a lower monthly payment, but taking double the time to pay off).

As for the question of whether or not you *should* by a house, aside from whether or not you can afford one, this happens to be a heavily debated topic. Here is a summary of the often-cited pros and cons of buying versus renting:

- **Flexibility**: Buying a home typically requires a large down payment and a long-term mortgage commitment. Renting, on the other hand, may have a lower upfront cost and offer more flexibility in terms of the length of the lease.

- **Financial stability**: Buying a home is a significant financial investment and requires a stable income and good credit. If you're not in a stable financial position, renting may be a better option.
- **Location**: Renting may be more attractive if you're not sure about your long-term plans or if you're looking to live in a specific area for a short period of time. If you're looking to settle down in one location for a longer period, buying a home in that area may be a better option.
- **Appreciation**: Buying a home can be a good investment as it can appreciate in value over time. Renting, on the other hand, doesn't provide the same financial benefit.
- **Maintenance**: When you own a home, you're responsible for all maintenance and repairs, which can be costly. Renting a home means the landlord is typically responsible for these costs.

Ultimately, when it comes to homeownership, it's important to weigh the pros and cons of both options and consider your personal circumstances and financial goals before making a decision. Many multimillionaires go their entire lives renting, and there are just as many who own their primary residence.

Tips to Build a Good Credit Score

Speaking of all these big purchases, let's talk a bit more about your credit score and how to get it higher. Remember, you want a higher credit score because you will typically get a lower interest rate on your loans. For example, if you are buying a house, just a 1% increase in your mortgage rate can mean that you will pay nearly $30,000 more in interest over the duration of the loan. Ouch!

Here are a few tips to help you build a better credit score:

- **Pay your bills on time**. Late payments can have a significant impact on your credit score. Make sure you pay all your bills on time, including credit cards, loans, and utility bills.

- **Keep your credit card balances low**. High credit card balances can indicate to lenders that you're overextending yourself financially and may be a higher risk for default. Keep your credit card balances low and pay them off in full each month if possible.

- **Limit new credit applications**. Every time you apply for credit, it shows up as a hard inquiry on your credit report, which can temporarily lower your score. Limit the number of new credit applications and only apply for credit when you truly need it.

- **Keep old credit accounts open**. A long credit history can be beneficial for your score. Keep old credit accounts open, even if you're not using them, as they can help to increase the length of your credit history.

- **Check your credit report**. Make sure to check your credit report regularly for errors. If you find any errors, dispute them with the credit bureau to have them corrected.

- **Diversify credit types**. Having a mix of different types of credit, such as credit cards, loans, and lines of credit, can be beneficial for your score. This shows lenders that you can handle different types of credit responsibly.

- **Be patient**. Building a good credit score takes time and effort. It's important to be patient and consistent with your efforts to improve your score.

Remember, a good credit score is important as it can impact your ability to qualify for loans, credit cards, and other financial products with favorable terms. It's also important to note that you should use credit responsibly and only borrow what you can afford to pay back.

Understanding Life Insurance

Life insurance can be a confusing topic. Essentially, life insurance is a contract between an individual and an insurance company. The individual pays a premium (a regular payment) to the insurance company, and in return, the insurance company provides a financial benefit to the individual's designated beneficiaries (usually family members) in the event of the individual's death.

The purpose of life insurance is to provide financial protection and security for your loved ones by ensuring they will have a source of income to replace what you were providing while you were alive. This can help them cover expenses such as mortgage payments, education costs, and everyday living expenses, so they can maintain their standard of living. A life insurance policy should not be a money-making scheme for you (despite what a salesperson may try to convince you). It should be there to provide peace of mind for those who depend on you should the unthinkable occur.

There are two main types of life insurance: term life insurance and whole life insurance. Term life insurance provides coverage for a specified period of time (let's say, twenty years) and pays a death benefit only if the individual dies during that time period. It is generally less expensive than whole life insurance.

Whole (also referred to as permanent) life insurance provides coverage for the individual's entire lifetime and also builds cash value over time. It is more expensive than term life insurance and also provides an investment and savings component.

When you purchase a life insurance policy, you will typically select the amount of coverage you want, which is known as the death benefit. This is the amount of money that will be paid to your beneficiaries if you pass away.

Regarding the question of which is better, term life or whole life, most experts recommend term life insurance for young adults. This is because term life insurance can last up to forty years and is five to fifteen times more affordable than permanent life insurance.

Any insurance policy that builds a cash value over time and is sold as an "investment" must underperform the investments it claims to hold in order to funnel some profits to the insurance company and pay commissions to its sales team. Basically, you would in many cases be much better off investing that extra money on your own.

Despite whatever benefits a salesperson may tout, know that nearly every policyholder of a universal life, variable life, whole life, or indexed universal life (IUL) insurance plan has paid a lot more money into it than it's currently worth. If you need life insurance because someone is depending on your income to live, buy an inexpensive term life insurance policy and continue to invest as much money as possible into real investments, like ETFs.

Also note, many employers automatically provide a basic level of life insurance—usually equivalent to about one year of your salary. In fact, you may not even know you have it, since many employers pay for this coverage on your behalf and do not deduct it from your paycheck. In that case you may not want to worry about getting a term life insurance policy until you have someone (like a child or spouse) depending on your income.

When that time comes, many experts will recommend you expand your policy coverage to equal ten to twelve times your annual income. So if you're making $50,000 a year, you have a young child, and your employer currently provides you with $100,000 worth of coverage, you should seek an additional $400,000 worth of coverage to take your total death benefit to at least $500,000.

Track Your Net Worth

Net worth was alluded to in chapter 4, but now let's break it down in a bit more detail. Think of your net worth as the dollar amount that would end up in your bank if you instantly sold everything you own: your car, house, stocks, bonds, baseball cards, wall art, whatever you have of value. However, you then have to subtract your debts (mortgage, credit card balances, student loans). What is left is your net worth. You will often hear people say "assets minus liabilities." Same thing.

Tracking your net worth is an important step in managing your personal finances, as it allows you to see your overall financial picture. By keeping track of your net worth, you can do the following:

- **Set financial goals**. Knowing your net worth can help you set realistic financial goals, such as saving for retirement or paying off debt.

- **Monitor progress**. By tracking your net worth over time, you can see how your financial situation is improving (or not) and make changes as necessary.
- **Identify areas for improvement**. By seeing where your assets and liabilities stand, you may identify areas where you can improve your finances, such as paying off high-interest debt or increasing contributions to your retirement savings.
- **Make better financial decisions**. By having a clear picture of your net worth, you'll be able to make more informed financial decisions. It allows you to evaluate the potential impact of actions such as buying a new car or taking on additional debt.
- **Get a sense of financial security**. Seeing your net worth grow over time can give you a sense of financial security and confidence. Knowing you have assets to fall back on can provide peace of mind and help you sleep better at night.

My own hot take—your net worth is way more important than your income. GASP! "But when I talk about money with my friends, we compare salaries. We talk about raises. We go after jobs that give us higher pay and fancy job titles," you might say.

Look, the amount of money that you make is a very important part of your overall financial situation, but it doesn't tell the full story. However, your net worth does.

It is important to track your net worth because it takes a wide view and looks at the whole picture. Looking only at your assets probably makes you feel good, but in reality, you also need to look at liabilities (debts) to put those assets into perspective. Some of the people you know who earn more money than you quite possibly do not have a higher net worth than you because they spend all their income on stuff—and not stuff that goes up in value.

I personally find that tracking my net worth is very motivating, and I typically check it every month or so. And since I've started watching my net worth, I think long and hard before I do something: "Will this make my net worth go up or down?"

When you start tracking, you will realize how day-to-day decision-making can impact the trajectory of your net worth, and when you look back in one year, five years, or ten years at how far you've come, you will experience that priceless sense of accomplishment.

> *If your net worth isn't changing, change your network.*
>
> — Grant Cardone, renowned sales trainer
> and investor

You could track your net worth on a spreadsheet, but it starts to get old very quickly (trust me, I've done it). Once your number of investment accounts, savings accounts, credit cards, for example, continue to grow, there are a lot of numbers involved. I moved to Empower (formerly Personal Capital) and haven't looked back since. The dashboard is intuitive, and once you link all your accounts, it will even analyze your investment portfolio for you and let you know how your returns compare against the major market indices (like the Dow and S&P 500).

As of this writing, Empower is free to use, but if they see that your assets are above a certain amount, they will ask to manage it for you for a fee (which I politely declined, because I am clearly enjoying managing my money on my own for the time being).

Figure 15 provides a screenshot of my own Empower dashboard as of this book's publication. As you can see, it is very sleek and easy to understand.

Figure 15: Sample Dashboard for Net Worth Tracking

Disclaimer: I may or may not get a small referral bonus if you use the QR code to sign up for Empower. Use my link if you'd like, or just Google it and go from there, or use an Excel spreadsheet. Whatever floats your boat. Point is, start tracking your net worth ASAP so that you can clearly see where you've come from and steer toward where you want to be.

Scan to start tracking your net worth with **Empower**

When to Hire a Financial Advisor

I hope you've found the content in this book to be clear, concise, and actionable. However, I obviously was unable to account for the infinite possibilities of your unique financial situation when writing it. For areas where you may be confused, I recommend the tried-and-true method of performing a Google search.

You'll find abundant resources on up-to-date account regulations, tax strategies, and general financial advice on blogs and other online resources. If that still doesn't answer your questions, or if you've simply become too busy with other aspects of life to spend time optimizing your finances, it may be time to consider hiring a financial advisor.

There are several other circumstances in which you might consider hiring a financial advisor:

- **When you have a significant amount of assets to manage**: If you have a large amount of savings, investments, and other assets, it can be beneficial to work with a financial advisor to help you manage and grow your wealth.
- **When you're approaching retirement**: As you near retirement, it's important to have a plan in place to ensure you have enough money to live on during your golden years. A financial advisor can help you create a retirement plan that takes into account your projected income, expenses, and lifestyle goals.
- **When you're facing a major life event**: Major life events such as getting married, having children, or buying a house can have a significant impact on your finances. A financial advisor can help you navigate these changes and create a plan to achieve your financial goals.
- **When you're not confident in your own ability to manage your finances**: If you're not confident in your ability to make sound financial decisions, it might be beneficial to

work with a financial advisor who can guide you through the process.

- **When you want to get a second opinion**: Even if you feel comfortable managing your finances on your own, it can be helpful to work with a financial advisor to get a second opinion on your financial plan and make sure you're on track to achieve your goals.

Just remember, financial advisors charge fees, and just a 2% fee (which is typical for clients with a low net worth) can eat up millions of dollars in future value over a lifetime of investing. So how do you find a good financial advisor? To quote Personal Finance Club's Jeremy Schneider, "I can't tell you how to distinguish between a good financial advisor and a bad one without teaching you how to invest. And once you know that much, you may not need a financial advisor at all."

Typically, investment growth is not achieved through expert stock selection and trading, but rather through purchasing and retaining stocks and allowing market growth to drive returns.

Now that you have made it through this chapter, you likely realize what I meant by my claim that this is where finance begins to get personal. We saw lots of twists and turns and "do this if you have this, but not if you have that" throughout the various sections. The bottom line is that you should do your research before you make any big money decisions.

This book is a great start, but it would likely be a good idea to dig deeper into topics that are still a bit hazy for you. If you find yourself overwhelmed with the options, there is no harm in hiring a financial advisor to get up to speed on your life and situation and then recommend tailored actions. Check out

www.Garrettplanningnetwork.com and **www.ameriprise.com** as good places to start. They offer online screeners to narrow down a list of financial advisors depending on what your needs are.

As stated, they will charge you a fee for this service, but it could be worth it depending on how complicated your situation is. Investing and paying a fee is still better than not investing at all. At the same time, again, being educated on these matters does help to understand what is going on, and you probably didn't learn any of it in school. So read blogs, check out more books, and listen to personal finance podcasts. There are a ton of resources out there to expand your new foundation.

Key Takeaways

- Evaluate putting excess money into HSAs and 529s as additional ways to optimize your taxes and grow your wealth.
- Start setting aside money for large, near-term savings goals.
- Begin tracking your net worth on a monthly basis to view your progress.

Take Action: Car Affordability Worksheet

If you are in the market for a new car, use the prompts in this worksheet to get a rough idea of just how much you can afford. Note: These calculations are rough estimates and may not reflect your individual financial situation. It is important to consider other factors such as the interest rate, down payment, and insurance when determining what you can afford to spend on a car.

How much can I afford to spend on a car?

Monthly Take-Home Pay: $_____

Max Car Loan Payment **(Monthly Take-Home Pay x 10%)**: $_____
*Note that your max total monthly car expenses, including loan (above), plus gas, insurance, and maintenance should be no more than your **Monthly Take-Home Pay x 20%**.

Now that you know approximately how much you can spend each month on a car loan, plug the amount into an online calculator (you can find many with a quick search). Be prepared to be asked to input the following information:

- Proposed monthly payment (from above calculation)
- Proposed loan term (the shorter the loan, the less you pay in interest)
- Estimated credit score
- Whether you are looking at new cars or used (impacts loan interest rate)

The calculator will present you with the maximum total amount that your monthly payment allows you to finance. Add in any down payment or trade-in value of your existing vehicle to arrive at your total budget. As you shop, remember that you'll have to pay sales tax, license, registration, and other fees out of this amount.

My proposed loan term:_____months

My credit score estimate:_____

My max monthly payment allows me to finance (per calculator): $_____

Total budget = down payment + trade-in equity + financeable amount = $_____

Want a free printable copy of this worksheet?
Visit investnowplaylater.com/worksheets

Start Early | End Early

Congratulations, that's it! You have made it through the seven pillars of money management. However, you now have to take action. It's time to start turning your next few paychecks into your first million dollars.

At the beginning of your personal finance journey, the biggest impact on your growth will be how significantly you can reduce your spending, and thus how far you can push the bar on your savings. As you progress, however, the biggest impact on your growth will transform into how much income you bring in. Pivoting into new income streams as you age, ideally passive ones, will go a long way in unlocking your financial freedom.

Along this journey, know that you will sometimes feel immense pressure to keep up with your friends, influencers, and the whims of our consumeristic society (in other words, you will feel the need to spend all your money just to keep up with everyone else).

Zig While Others Zag

Going out every night is a constant, yet costly, desire for many young adults your age. These entertainment expenses are discretionary; however, if you are dedicated to achieving financial health, getting rid of debt, and retiring as early as possible, it is best to keep discretionary spending to an absolute minimum, especially until your moderate- and high-interest debts are paid off. It's okay to let loose every once in a while, but informed decision-making (paired with common sense) can be a great tool to employ while forming a healthy financial strategy.

You can make a decision here. Do you want to live it up now and put your financial future at risk? Or are you willing to start zigging while everyone else is zagging? Saving while everyone else is spending? Investing in appreciating assets while everyone else is investing in depreciating assets? Planning while everyone else is partying?

If you feel like you have been zagging and are a part of the latter group, you are certainly in the majority. However, don't be too hard on yourself. Take the lessons in this book as a nudge in the right direction and, most importantly, stay the course, even if you experience a hiccup every once in a while.

The Time to Start Is Now

The sooner you begin working on these steps, the quicker you'll reach financial independence. In the same vein, the less money you spend on nonessentials and wants, the more you'll be able to allocate toward these goals and the quicker you'll progress through them. The harder you make each paycheck work, the quicker you'll stop having to work for one.

In summary, recall the major financial moves I covered and attack them in this order:

1. Budget, reduce expenses, and set realistic goals
2. Build an emergency fund

3. Max out your employer-matched savings plan
4. Pay down high-interest debt
5. Begin saving for retirement in an IRA
6. Accelerate retirement savings and plan your financial independence
7. Save for other goals and deploy advanced methods

And when investing, recall that it really is as simple as choosing one to five low-cost index funds, ideally diversified across US stocks, international stocks, and maybe some bonds. Turn on your dividend reinvestment setting within your accounts. Set up automatic investments where you can. Rebalance on a schedule as you age (that is, fewer stocks and more bonds as you get older, to limit risk). And lastly, don't sell anything until you retire, whether that be at age sixty-five or at age thirty-five.

Giving Back

Let's wrap up with a topic that has not been discussed much yet—giving and generosity. The preceding chapters focused heavily on the accumulation of wealth and achievement of financial freedom, but as we know, this is not all there is to life.

Donating time and money to support causes we are passionate about is, for many people, an important ingredient to overall happiness and fulfillment. One can undoubtedly make a bigger impact when they have control of their finances and are able to direct the fruits of their investments as they see fit.

It's also worth noting that once you reach a point of financial freedom where you no longer have to actively work to pay your bills, you unlock the greatest gift: time. If you so choose, this time could be spent focusing on making the world a better place.

Next Steps

Here is what I recommend you do now. At the end of this book, you will find a handy decision-making road map that summarizes the actions discussed in this book. Treat it almost as a waterfall and picture each of your paychecks starting at the top of the chart. Allow the money to flow down the steps until there is nothing left over; you will fill up each bucket with cash along the way before you can move to the next one underneath.

These steps are widely accepted throughout the personal finance community as the optimal path for most young people to follow, but of course a quick disclaimer—this will not always be the best route for everyone. Consult with a licensed professional if you are unsure of your situation.

If you ever get hung up on a box or cannot recall the reasoning behind an action, the associated chapter numbers are conveniently cited for you so that rereading a section is an easy way to gain clarity.

An investment in knowledge always pays the best interest.

— Benjamin Franklin,
Founding Father of the United States

Also, please continue to educate yourself about personal finance whenever possible. Read other books and articles to gain different perspectives, research available financial products, and keep apprised of changes in tax law. The best way to guarantee your financially secure future is to build knowledge that will form the baseline from which you can continue to make informed decisions.

I wish you the best of luck on your journey. Oh, and don't forget, the earlier you start, the earlier you reach your goals.

If you **Invest Hard Now**, you can **Play Hard Later**.

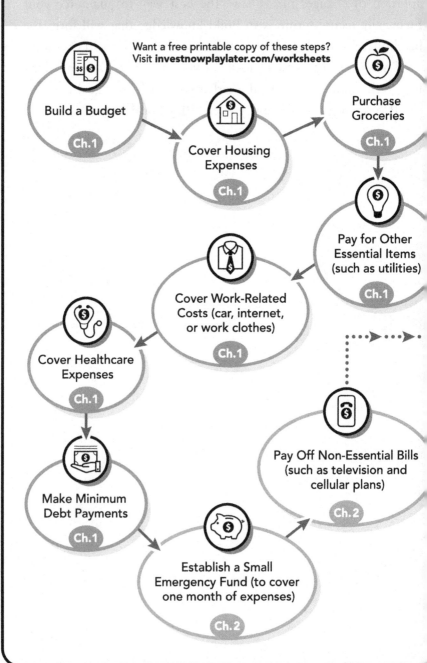

PERSONAL FINANCE
ROAD MAP FOR YOUNG ADULTS

Want a free printable copy of these steps?
Visit **investnowplaylater.com/worksheets**

Build a Budget
Ch.1

Cover Housing Expenses
Ch.1

Purchase Groceries
Ch.1

Pay for Other Essential Items (such as utilities)
Ch.1

Cover Work-Related Costs (car, internet, or work clothes)
Ch.1

Cover Healthcare Expenses
Ch.1

Make Minimum Debt Payments
Ch.1

Pay Off Non-Essential Bills (such as television and cellular plans)
Ch.2

Establish a Small Emergency Fund (to cover one month of expenses)
Ch.2

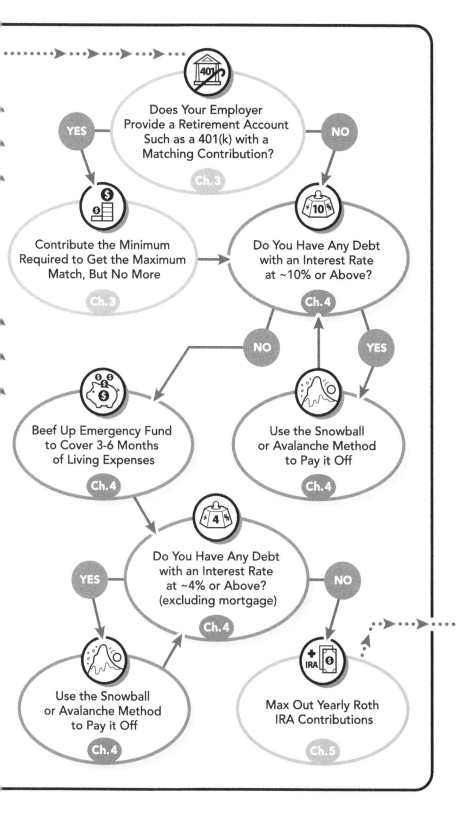

Does Your Employer Provide a Retirement Account Such as a 401(k) with a Matching Contribution?
Ch. 3

YES

NO

Contribute the Minimum Required to Get the Maximum Match, But No More
Ch. 3

Do You Have Any Debt with an Interest Rate at ~10% or Above?
Ch. 4

NO

YES

Beef Up Emergency Fund to Cover 3-6 Months of Living Expenses
Ch. 4

Use the Snowball or Avalanche Method to Pay it Off
Ch. 4

Do You Have Any Debt with an Interest Rate at ~4% or Above? (excluding mortgage)
Ch. 4

YES

NO

Use the Snowball or Avalanche Method to Pay it Off
Ch. 4

Max Out Yearly Roth IRA Contributions
Ch. 5

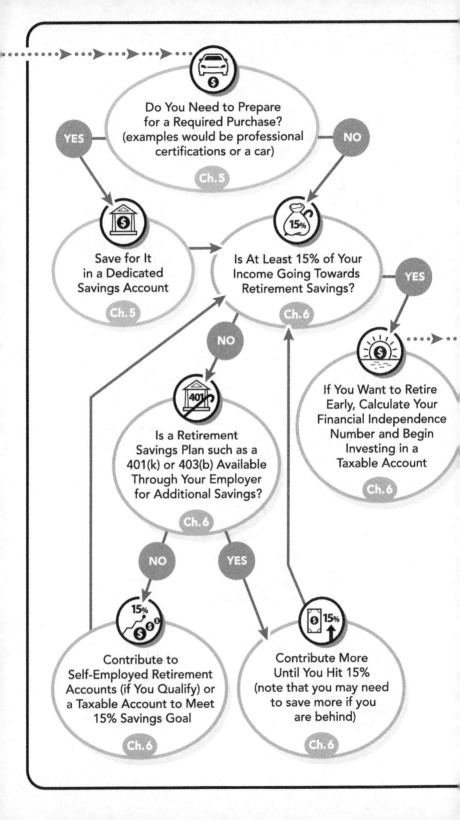

Do You Need to Prepare for a Required Purchase? (examples would be professional certifications or a car)
Ch. 5

YES

NO

Save for It in a Dedicated Savings Account
Ch. 5

Is At Least 15% of Your Income Going Towards Retirement Savings?
Ch. 6

YES

NO

If You Want to Retire Early, Calculate Your Financial Independence Number and Begin Investing in a Taxable Account
Ch. 6

Is a Retirement Savings Plan such as a 401(k) or 403(b) Available Through Your Employer for Additional Savings?
Ch. 6

NO

YES

Contribute to Self-Employed Retirement Accounts (if You Qualify) or a Taxable Account to Meet 15% Savings Goal
Ch. 6

Contribute More Until You Hit 15% (note that you may need to save more if you are behind)
Ch. 6

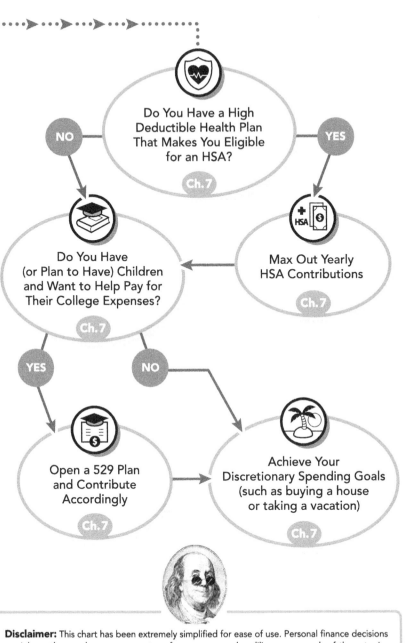

Do You Have a High Deductible Health Plan That Makes You Eligible for an HSA? Ch.7

NO → **Do You Have (or Plan to Have) Children and Want to Help Pay for Their College Expenses?** Ch.7

YES → **Max Out Yearly HSA Contributions** Ch.7 → **Do You Have (or Plan to Have) Children and Want to Help Pay for Their College Expenses?**

YES → **Open a 529 Plan and Contribute Accordingly** Ch.7

NO → **Achieve Your Discretionary Spending Goals (such as buying a house or taking a vacation)** Ch.7

References

To view the full list of sources referenced in this book, go to:
investnowplaylater.com/references.

Acknowledgments

I would like to express my heartfelt gratitude to the following individuals who have contributed immensely to the development of this book.

First, I extend my sincere thanks to John Aldridge, Jacques Bienvenu, Taylar Boutte, Grace Carrell Cuillier, Kelly Derise, Martha Do, Dan Herron, Nicholas Kilchrist, Maci Kraemer, Torie Laiche, Dave LeCount, Merrylue Martin, Christine Matzen, Patrick Mitchell, Luis Perez Gonzalez, Carter Pesson, Cheyenne Rambo, Nika Schrauf, and Jane Villermin. These beta readers provided invaluable feedback on the earlier drafts, pointed out confusing material, and highlighted areas that required further simplification. Without their input, this book would not have been as clear and effective for the intended audience.

I am also deeply grateful to my parents, whose unwavering support and constructive criticism helped me stay focused throughout the writing process and refine the content into its final form. Thank you for your help in making this series a success.

About the Author

L uke Villermin opened a retirement account and started investing in the stock market when he was fifteen. His only regret? That he didn't start earlier.

Since then, he has become the best-selling author of the Invest Now Play Later series and has shared his investing knowledge on multiple podcasts and interviews. At twenty-eight, Luke achieved financial independence through passive investments covering his living expenses.

When he isn't working his corporate day job or advocating financial literacy for young people, you can find him hiking, camping, and traveling to new places.

Visit his website at **lukevillermin.com**. He loves to hear from readers.

Did this book help you in some way?

Please consider leaving an honest review online so that others can find it as well.

Scan to be directed to the Amazon.com review submission site:

Your feedback is much appreciated. Thank you.

The Invest Now Play Later Series

Help your younger siblings kickstart their own investing habits by sharing these books with them.

A Teenager's Guide to Investing in the Stock Market is designed for those thirteen to eighteen years old. It dives deeper into the world of investing and provides a step-by-step road map to setting up the correct online account, purchasing stock, and putting money to work. Readers will learn about index funds, mutual funds, ETFs, and more!

On Your Mark, Get Set, INVEST is geared for kids ages eight to twelve and provides over a dozen interactive worksheets, fun illustrations, and kid-friendly examples to simplify the essential concepts of money management and personal finance, all while learning from the money decisions of Ritzy Rabbit and Thrifty Tortoise as they race to the finish line—at the end awaits a brand-new bike!

Scan to view the series on **Amazon.com**

Made in United States
Orlando, FL
09 December 2023